Deaf Daughter
Hearing Father

Deaf Daughter
Hearing Father

Richard Medugno

GALLAUDET UNIVERSITY PRESS
Washington, DC

Gallaudet University Press
Washington, D.C. 20002
http://gupress.gallaudet.edu

Printed in the United States of America

ISBN 1-56368-277-X

Library of Congress Cataloging-in-Publication Data

Medugno, Richard.
   Deaf daughter, hearing father / Richard Medugno.
      p. cm.
   Includes bibliographical references and index.
   ISBN 1-56368-277-X
   1. Medugno, Richard. 2. Medugno, Miranda Marisa, 1991– 3. Parents of deaf children—Canada—Biography. 4. Parents of deaf children—United States—Biography.
5. Deaf children—Canada—Biography. 6. Deaf children—United States—Biography.
7. Fathers and daughters—Biography. I. Title.

HQ759.913.M438 2005
306.874'0973—dc22

                                                                                2005046291

Book design and composition by John Reinhardt Book Design

For Brenda, Terence, and Miranda
The loves of my life

Contents

Introduction

WHEN I FIRST ENVISIONED *Deaf Daughter, Hearing Father* it was as a kind of a *Chicken Soup for the Parent of a Deaf Child*. I wanted to write short, pithy, and easily digestible pieces about my experience raising a deaf child. It was suggested to me by Gallaudet University Press editor Ivey Pittle Wallace that a narrative was required to tie all the separate "pearls" together to create a complete, satisfying work. I saw the wisdom in this and tackled the assignment with zest. I hope the personal story of my family is seen as informative, not self-indulgent.

I also hope the reader will ultimately find this book an uplifting and positive experience, as has been most of my time as the father of a deaf daughter. There have been disappointments and downers, which I have included in the book as well to give an accurate and honest view. I don't profess that this book is a be-all and end-all for raising a deaf child—a *Raising Deafies for Hearing Dummies*, if you will. I am not a know-it-all. I'm more like a know-it-small. I just know what it's been like for my family and me. Perhaps sharing our experiences will help guide or ease the load for other folks similarly confronted, or enlighten and entertain those who are interested in the lives of deaf children and the Deaf community.

When I first learned that my daughter was profoundly deaf, I read many books; one that I appreciated a good deal was *Deaf Like Me* written by Thomas S. Spradley and James P. Spradley. Published in the 1970s, it was dated by the time I read it in the early 1990s. I appreciated the anecdotal experiences detailed in the book by the father about his young hearing family and his deaf daughter. I would be overjoyed if *Deaf Daughter, Hearing Father* were to be regarded by others as highly as *Deaf Like Me*.

I've learned a few helpful things in the past decade or so that I want to share; but mostly what I hope to accomplish with this book is to give parents of newly identified deaf children, particularly fathers, access to my experiences and a real idea about what it means to have a deaf child in the family.

Hopefully, this information will provide perspective, help other parents avoid my pitfalls, and provide a bit of guidance on how to raise a kid who has a different communication mode than the rest of the family.

Ultimately, the message I want to convey in this book is that there are numerous challenges for a hearing parent with a deaf child; but facing the obstacles will lead to rewards that will be far greater than any you have ever hoped for or could have imagined.

RAM
Fremont, California
November 2004

Chapter One

Palindrome

THE STORY OF HAVING A DEAF DAUGHTER truly begins for me in 1990, more than a year before she was born. I was a thirty-one-year-old American, living with my Canadian wife, Brenda Paddon, and our year-old son, Terence, in Toronto, Ontario, Canada. I was working for the Ontario Medical Association in an administrative support job that paid the rent but did not satisfy my heart and soul. I had a B.A. degree in drama from the University of California, Irvine, and a dream of being a professional playwright.

I had subscribed to the notion that I couldn't be both a family man and a successful dramatist, unless I became wildly successful overnight. So when Brenda and I married a few years before, I was prepared to settle down to a bourgeois lifestyle. It was not a difficult decision as I'd never been much of a bohemian, which I felt was necessary for a writer, at least, until the breakthroughs came. And I also felt some "real-life" experience could add depth and breadth to my writing. I entertained the idea that perhaps I could be another George Bernard Shaw, whose theatre career didn't start until he was fifty, or so the legend goes.

It should come as no surprise that after a couple of years of riding the subway to my office job, I would get restless and become dissatisfied with my employment situation. I sought some outside help. During the summer of 1990, I started seeing a career counselor who was of minimal assistance. I knew that I was a good writer; I just couldn't figure out how I could get paid enough to support a family. If I am completely honest here, I will confess that I did not believe in myself enough to chance it.

Then one night, I had a strange dream. There was really nothing to the dream but a word: palindrome. I literally woke up with palindrome on my mind. I had no clue what this word meant. I cracked my dictionary to learn that *palindrome* means a word, number, or phrase that reads the same backwards as forward. Examples of palindromes are *Otto* and *Anna* and *1881*.

Learning the definition of palindrome did not change my life immediately, but it did give me an odd sense of comfort, knowing or believing something was in the works. I began looking out for palindromes. It would take several years before the dream would make sense to me.

A few months after the dream, my wife informed me that she was pregnant. I am embarrassed to report that initially I was not very happy with the news. Having a second child only two years after our first seemed way too soon. However, I quickly warmed to the idea that our son Terence would soon have a playmate. Without much discussion with Brenda, I decided that after the birth of this child, if it were a healthy and normal baby, I would get a vasectomy.

The key words here are *healthy and normal*. For the longest time, I had the premonition that I would be the father of a child with a disability. I believe this premonition was rooted in feeling guilty. It stemmed from my brother Joe, who is a year older than I and mentally retarded. I felt badly because of the way I treated him when we were younger.

Joe, the oldest of the six of us, was born with brain damaged due to a lack of oxygen at birth. His disability is not so severe that he can't live by himself or hold down a job. However, his IQ is low and he cannot drive a car. In many ways, he is very much like a twelve-year-old boy in a man's body. He has a good heart and is beloved by his family, friends, neighbors, and coworkers.

As the second-oldest son, I had the responsibilities of the first but not the title. I suppose this resentment was natural, and I have long since gotten over it, but I had a past that couldn't forgive and forget. As a child and teenager, I was frequently embarrassed by and of my brother. In response, I was often mean and unhelpful to him. As an adult looking back, I realized the magnitude of my unpleasantness and felt remorseful. I suppose it was around this time when the premonition started; I felt I would have to face disability again in my life. I decided that if I did become the father of a disabled child, I would consider it an opportunity to redeem myself for the way I behaved with my brother.

Home Birth

On August 19, 1991, my daughter Miranda Marisa Medugno was born at our home in East York, Ontario. With three midwives in attendance, my wife Brenda and I pulled a beautiful baby out of a tiny womb and into this big world. Miranda was a perfect little baby girl, weighing six pounds, eleven ounces. Our son, Terence, was also in attendance for some of the birthing process. He was born two years earlier at a hospital in Toronto.

Terence was a healthy, normal baby as well, though his birth was not nearly as pleasant an experience for all concerned as Miranda's home birth was. Granted, this is a simplistic comparison, but we found that hospital staff had their own agendas and timetables, while the midwives were trained to let nature take its course and support the birth process, not hijack and turn it into a medical emergency.

It's important to note here that because of our experience with Terence in the hospital, we became less naive when dealing with professionals in medical settings. We don't accept every doctor's or nurse's statement as gospel truth. Having said that, we would not hesitate to seek assistance from medical professionals and risk our children's health or our own. Still, we considered a home birth with professional midwives less risky than a birth in a hospital. Miranda had no health-related issues from being born in the basement bedroom of our house on Queensdale Avenue.

In the fall of 1991, I took advantage of Ontario's family-friendly society and the newly instated paternity leave. I was able to take off work for three months at about 70 percent of my full salary and stay home with my wife and the kids. It was a good time, not having to rush off to the office and being able to stay home with my family and contemplate the future.

I took one week during this time off to have the vasectomy and recover. The actual procedure may have been quick and painless, but the aftermath of sitting around with an ice pack on my crotch for days I will never forget.

Miranda in a brat pack on my back at my in-law's home in Mississauga, Ontario, in early 1992, before we knew she was deaf.

I returned to work in December 1991 and for the next year or so, our family life proceeded as we expected it would. Having a baby and a two-year-old was hectic often, but Brenda and I have many fond memories that include double strollers and messy meal times. Miranda was colicky for a few months. I nicknamed her "Fussy." (I have a penchant for giving nicknames, a gift that is not always appreciated by recipients. Over the years, Miranda has been dubbed "Chubba, Panda, Dolly, The Girl," and "Our Little Deafie." When she was first born, Terence melded Miranda's name with his mother's and started calling the baby "Mirbrenda.")

Miranda grew and developed at a normal pace. Brenda always felt there was something a little different about our girl, but she couldn't put her finger on it and dismissed her concerns with the thought that "all babies are different." I, of course, being basically clueless, had no concerns whatsoever. At around nine or ten months of age, Brenda began to notice that Miranda was not vocalizing as Terence had. Miranda tended to whine. At her one-year checkup, Brenda mentioned to the doctor that Miranda seemed not to be hearing, because she wasn't responding when we called her name. The physician did a cursory check and thought there was nothing with which to be concerned. He did not recommend a hearing test, saying Miranda was too young. Later, we found out this was untrue.

Nowadays, in many locales, newborns are given auditory brain stem tests as part of the battery of tests that they receive; these tests are not invasive or painful and give an immediate picture of the baby's hearing capabilities. All new parents should have this test administered to their babies because the sooner you find out the child is deaf, the sooner you can begin to focus on visually communicating.

As the months passed and our daughter's vocabulary did not consist of any words, our concerns began to grow. We started testing Miranda, finding that sometimes she would respond, and other times she would not. I have a distinct memory of getting down on all fours and growling like a bear to a crawling Miranda. And she mimicked my growl exactly. "She couldn't do that if she were deaf, could she?" I remember asking myself that later when confronted by the possibility of her being deaf.

Brenda made an appointment with a specialist at Toronto's Hospital for Sick Children. During the time between making the appointment and going, I recall walking through the busy downtown Toronto inter-section of Yonge and Bloor during my lunch hour and seeing a couple of deaf teenagers signing. A chill, colder than the Canadian winter wind blowing down Yonge Street, went up and down my spine. Honestly, I was horrified that my daughter could be like "one of them."

Though I had never met a deaf person in my life, or at least, I don't remember ever meeting one, I wasn't completely unexposed to the Deaf community. I remember seeing the play *Children of a Lesser God* per-formed by the San Diego Repertory Theatre a few years before. I also saw the movie version with Marlee Matlin and William Hurt. I do recall tak-ing note of the Gallaudet University student rebellion in March of 1988 and feeling supportive of them. However, now with the "threat" that my daughter might be one of them, I could only think of all the things that would be unavailable to her in life. I was focused on what she couldn't do. Or rather, what I thought she wouldn't be able to do. I did not ruminate on these notions long, as it was too painful, and I held on to the hope that if she had a hearing problem, it could probably be fixed.

A few days before the big doctor's appointment, I came home from work to find my mother-in-law, Barbara Paddon, visiting. When I en-tered our house, Miranda had her back to the door. She did not see me and was preoccupied with a toy. Barbara asked what I thought about the baby's hearing problems. I said, "Well, there's something wrong." Then I stepped behind Miranda and clapped my hands really hard. She did not jump or flinch or acknowledge my presence in any way. "Yep, we sure have a problem," I thought.

The Diagnosis

In January of 1993, when she was seventeen months old, Brenda packed Miranda and her brother off to the Hospital for Sick Children in downtown Toronto for testing by an audiologist. I went to my office and anxiously waited for a phone call. I don't know why I didn't accompany Brenda and the kids to the hospital, except perhaps because I sensed I would have a tough time in public, if the news came back "bad." Finally, Brenda did phone with the news, saying something to the effect that our suspicions have been confirmed. I knew there would be a problem; I just wondered about the severity.

Brenda said the hearing loss was quite severe. She explained how the audiologist placed them all in a soundproof room, with Miranda sitting in the middle of the room, playing with toys, and Brenda and Terence sitting behind Miranda. The audiologist piped in tones of high and low frequency, and Miranda rarely looked up to see what "the sound was." Increasing the volume on the sounds caused Brenda and Terence to squirm and plug their ears in pain, while Miranda continued to play with her toys "blissfully unaware," as they say. The diagnosis was profound sensorineural bilateral deafness. The professionals suspected it was a genetic defect and present at birth.

Obviously, Brenda was upset by the diagnosis, but she was also relieved. She finally understood what was "different" about Miranda. I, on the other hand, was devastated. When I hung up the phone, I closed my office door, put my head on my desk, and wept. Later that day, as I was giving the news to some of my coworkers, several times I was misunderstood and people thought I was saying, "My daughter's dead." It felt that way, until I saw her again and held her in my arms.

That evening, I met my wife and kids at my in-laws' home. When I came through the door, Terence and Miranda were running around. I picked Miranda up, hugged her tightly, and cried again, while three-year-old Terence informed me, "Miranda's ears are broke." Miranda, uncomfortable with my firm embraced, squirmed out of my arms, and when she was back on solid ground, she tore after her brother and the chase was on again.

Later that night, I called my parents in California and broke the news. Since they had dealt with my brother Joe's disability, I knew they would appreciate some of what I was feeling and have good advice. After expressing their disappointment and concern, they simply said, "Things will get better. It's not the end of the world." They did and it wasn't.

So what about my "palindrome" dream? I believe now that it refers to the year 1991, the year when Miranda was born. Having a deaf daughter was a major turning point for me. It changed the direction of my life—for the better.

Chapter Two

"So How Are You Planning to Communicate with Your Little Girl?"

As one would expect, the first few months after Miranda's diagnosis were eventful and difficult. I believe Elizabeth Kubler-Ross's stages of grief are applicable to parents finding out they have a deaf (or disabled) child: denial, anger, bargaining, depression, and acceptance. I certainly experienced each of these stages.

With the diagnosis, it was not the imminent death of our child, but the immediate death of the dreams we had for that child that we had to grieve. No question, we had our tough times, but I believe Brenda and I moved through the stages pretty darn quickly.

I'm not sure why, but perhaps, for myself, it was the fact that I had a mentally disabled brother. Another thing that helped me adjust quickly was hearing awful stories about parents who did not accept their child's deafness. I didn't want to ever be accused of handicapping my child with my own hang-up about acceptance.

Though we mourned the loss of our "hearing daughter" and the dreams of a blond pixie with big brown eyes who would play duets on the piano with her mom and sing silly songs with her dad, we could now take some positive action. New visions began to bloom in our heads and new feelings blossomed in our hearts for our Miranda.

Making Contact

The first conscious visual communication I had with Miranda happened within a few days of learning that she was deaf. In our kitchen, she stood up on a chair wearing only her diaper and plastic pants. With her curly blond hair, round face, and big brown eyes, all she needed was a pair of wings to become a cherub and take flight. I gestured for her to sit down and was quite surprised when she lowered herself. When she rose again, I motioned again for her to sit down. Again, she did. There was such satisfaction in this simple exchange.

In subsequent medical appointments, it was conveyed to us that with hearing aids and speech therapy, a deaf child could learn to speak and achieve a certain "normalcy." Brenda and I started doing a lot of research. We read whatever we could get our hands on about raising a deaf child. I remember reading a case history about how a little girl with a similar diagnosis should be able to develop normal speech and language skills and attend regular school. Once hearing aids were put on, she would instantly begin to develop verbal language. In six weeks, she would say her first word: "Mama."

I remember optimistically showing my in-laws the scenario. This case history raised expectations about this little girl of ours becoming "normal." I was cautiously optimistic. It took some time to get the hearing aids and earmolds for Miranda. It wasn't a pleasant experience for Brenda to take our daughter around to all the appointments with the specialists.

Brenda recalled that the hearing aid consultant, an older chap named Pete Keller, offered without being asked, "There's no Deaf community. It's just a bunch of deaf people standing around signing." In retrospect, we are horrified that a person with such a bias is one of the first "experts" that parents with newly diagnosed parents would see. This negativity about the Deaf community was very much the prevailing attitude with medical and quasi-medical professionals we had contact with in Toronto in 1993.

When we received the hearing aids, it was not easy to put them in Miranda's ears and keep her pudgy, baby fingers from pulling them out. The high-pitched whistle of a misfit or recently removed hearing aid is also not a fond memory. Once while visiting my Auntie Sue in Boston, we had to turn her house upside down looking for Miranda's hearing aids. My aunt is a seamstress who works out of her home, consequently there are stacks of clothing all around. Our two-and-a-half-year-old girl had taken her hearing aids out and stuck them under a pile of clothes, where they didn't whistle until someone moved the pile.

After several months of using hearing aids, it was very clear that Miranda Panda wasn't going to be like the child who suddenly became a "normal" kid after getting her hearing aids. This was somewhat disappointing. We were, of course, told that improvement would not occur overnight. Months went by, but we saw very little improvement in Miranda's ability to attend to sound. After a year, we decided the hearing aids were unnecessary. Miranda did learn to say, "Mama." But that was a few years later, long after she'd given up wearing hearing aids.

We did not wait until our daughter could "hear" or "speak" or had hearing aids to start communicating with her. Within days of the diagnosis, assuming that it was only natural for deaf people to sign, we started to learn American Sign Language (ASL). Our initiative was rewarded almost instantaneously. Miranda responded to our gestures and elementary signs by mimicking us. Soon, instead of whining, she was signing! And the more she did of the latter, the less she did of the former.

Hearing Assessment Program

Three months after the initial diagnosis, the Hospital for Sick Children in Toronto had Miranda go through the Hearing Assessment Program (HAP). During a period of three consecutive days, the young child sees a team of specialists from each of the following departments: Otolaryngology, Audiology, Pediatrics, Auditory Training, Psychology, Speech, Ophthalmology, Social Work, CT Scan, Education, and Public Health.

After all the specialists have seen him or her, they come together at the end of the week to discuss the child's prognosis with the parents. Miranda certainly did not enjoy three days being tested, poked, and prodded by people in white coats. On the third day, she began getting upset anytime she saw a person in a white lab coat approaching.

The HAP didn't tell us much more that we had already known: Miranda had been profoundly deaf since birth; this was caused by an unknown reason, most likely, a recessive gene. Simply, her hearing did not develop "normally." It would be difficult, though not impossible, for her to learn to "listen" and "speak."

Perhaps the most interesting aspect of the meetings was the lack of a single deaf representative in the group of specialists, though there was a teacher who provided information concerning "the auditory-verbal approach to educating hearing impaired children." Fortunately, we did receive *The Parent Sharing Kit,* written and published by the Canadian Hearing Society, from the hospital's social worker. The kit contained a folder full of information about the resources available for parents of deaf children.

Itinerant Teachers

Shortly after the diagnosis, we began to receive home visits from a teacher of the deaf provided by the Toronto Board of Education. The first teacher to visit us was named Joyce. She was a kind, supportive, hearing person who would come over once a week for an hour with a bag full of educational toys. She sat and played with Miranda. "Learning through play" was the approach. Miranda seemed to enjoy these visits.

I believe at this point we were confronted with the communication choice for Miranda's education: oral or Total Communication. We didn't know a lot yet, but we leaned towards Total Communication because it made the most sense: use all methods of communication available, including signing, voicing, lipreading, listening with aids, and so on. So during sessions with Miranda, Joyce would sign and voice mostly nouns. One of other goals of the visits was to teach Brenda and me how to interact with and teach Miranda.

As I was working during the majority of Joyce's visits, Brenda was the parent who received the training. One auditory therapy exercise had Miranda sitting with her back to the teacher who had a glass bottle. Then the teacher would drop toys or small items into the bottle, creating a sound to which the student is supposed to react. The idea behind the exercise is to get the child to attend to the sound even if she can barely discern its occurrence.

"It's not a bad exercise," said Brenda. "But for us, it was a waste of time because Miranda was profoundly deaf. Of course we didn't know that at the time. An audiogram with children that young is hard to get accurate. So it may be a good thing to do with other deaf children, but for us, it wasn't much use. And Joyce wanted us to do it for a half-hour every day. For Miranda, it wasn't interesting enough, and it is difficult enough keeping any two-year-old's attention for even 5 minutes, let alone 30."

After only a few months, because we indicated a preference for a Total Communication approach and Joyce didn't have great signing skills, we started receiving visits from another teacher. Lee was a hearing woman who was married to a deaf man. Though we were at first excited to have a more fluent signer working with Miranda, ultimately Lee was a big disappointment. She was one of those professionals you run into who likes being "the expert" and telling the uneducated or uninformed what they're doing wrong. This was a big problem for us because Lee tended to undermine our confidence, particularly with our nascent signing skills.

In addition to that, Lee didn't know her boundaries and often tried to tell us how to parent (not only with our daughter but our son as well!). Ironically, and perhaps not surprisingly, this was an area she had no expertise in, since she was childless. Needless to say, Lee really rubbed us the wrong way. Her style was invasive and abrasive. Ultimately, we felt she did more harm than good for us.

When Miranda started going to the Happy Hands preschool at the Bob Rumball Centre for the Deaf (BRCD) in the summer, home visits with Lee were moved to after-school sessions at BRCD one afternoon a week. The relationship between Lee and Brenda did not improve there.

Brenda said of Lee, "She would do things like this: I'd have some plastic colored eggs, and I would sign to Miranda: BROWN EGG. Then Lee would jump in and say, 'No, no. You can't sign that. It's a tan egg. You'll confuse the child.' Now, with my hearing son, I probably would have said, 'brown,' but she just had to jump in and show she was in charge."

Things finally came to a head and Brenda told Lee off and put an end to the superfluous and counterproductive lessons. Unfortunately, although we have had mostly good experiences with professionals regarding Miranda, we have had our share of negative ones. Typically, it is the insensitive remark like an audiologist asking Brenda, when Miranda was throwing a "terrible-two" fit, "Who's in charge? The parent or the child?" Again, the audiologist was childless at the time and had no idea what a two-year-old is like on a full-time basis.

Sign Language Classes at Home

Shortly after Miranda's diagnosis, we contacted Silent Voice, a nonprofit service organization for the deaf and their families in the Toronto area. They provided early intervention services like in-home sign language classes free of charge for families of newly diagnosed deaf children. A few weeks later, on a Saturday, a young, attractive Deaf woman showed up at our home. Her name was Jessica. She was the first deaf person, other than our daughter, that I'd ever met. She communicated in four languages fluently: ASL, English (reading, voicing), Mexican Sign Language, and Spanish (reading, voicing). She began by teaching the whole family signs around the house.

The following week, she came with a friend, another young Deaf woman whose name escapes me now. This friend kept the children busy while Jessica taught signs to Brenda and me. This went on for a couple of months, and we really appreciated the introduction to sign language and the Deaf community on our own turf. Soon I enrolled into a sign language class at the BRCD, going every Thursday evening for a couple of hours.

A Visit with a Deaf Family

Another helpful service that Silent Voice provided families like ours with was the opportunity to meet a deaf family, to give us more of an idea what successful deaf adults are like and how they live in the hearing world. Contrary to Pete Keller's observation, Brenda and I were discovering that there is a Deaf culture, and that the deaf people in it are quite happy being who and how they were. To the members of the Deaf community, deafness is not a disability. That idea was very intriguing to us.

Imagine having a disability but not feeling like you are disabled. It sounded like a great approach if one wanted to raise a child to be psychologically well balanced and self-confident. So we made the request to meet a deaf family.

Alfred and Shira and their two deaf sons arrived one Sunday afternoon for a visit with our little family. We were quite excited to have them come into our home. The kids played nicely as we got to know the couple, using our beginning sign language skills, their voicing and speechreading skills, and a good old-fashioned paper and pencil to communicate.

Alfred had a white-collar job working for the provincial government, and Shira, at the time, was a stay-at-home mom. They were warm and friendly. They drove a car and rented a house. It seemed they did just about everything our family did. It was an eye-opening experience. Being deaf certainly wasn't the horror show that I had imagined it to be.

Communication Choices

"So how are you planning to communicate with your little girl?" This question began to come up frequently in conversations. I remember discussing this with Alfred after he asked. At the time, I didn't fully realize how important a question that was. We seemed to have three communication choices before us: oralism, Total Communication, or manualism. As I understood it, oralism proposed that deaf kids could learn to hear and talk without the need for learning sign language (or the Deaf community!). However, in order to succeed, it was stressed that Miranda would have to spend years going to speech therapists and other specialists.

As is my nature, I was skeptical after being told I could have a "normal" kid if I just did whatever the professionals told us to do. (As an employee of the Ontario Medical Association, I had a lot of contact with physicians and knew that they were mere mortals, not the all-knowing gods and goddesses of medicine many of them would like to be seen as.)

The Total Communication option seemed to make a lot of sense to me. This option called for the use of all the communication methods available: sign, speak, lipread, listen, gesture, mime, and, of course, write. In practice, this is what most deaf people do in the real world. As a mode for teaching deaf children, Total Communication in the classroom is often called Sim-Com (for Simultaneous Communication) where voicing English and signing are done at the same time. Because ASL is not English, an invented sign system called S.E.E. (Signing Exact English) is used.

I was quite disappointed when Alfred expressed to me his belief that Total Communication wasn't a good approach. I learned from him that most Deaf people considered S.E.E. a corruption of the beauty and efficiency of ASL. Alfred felt that manualism was the best option for people who were profoundly deaf from birth like himself and our Miranda. I began to hear that repeatedly from Deaf people, most of whom had been raised with the oralism or Total Communication approaches.

Manualism in a school setting is now supported by an educational philosophy called bi-bi, short for bilingual and bicultural. This philosophy has two basic tenets. The first idea is that ASL and English are different languages and should be treated and taught as such. The second idea is that deaf and hearing people inhabit different cultural spheres. At the time, I found this hard to understand and accept; but with repeated exposure, I have certainly found this to be true.

Conference on Deaf Mental Health Issues

In May of 1995, I attended the fifteenth annual conference of the Ontario Council on Deaf Mental Health Issues held at the University of Toronto. I was part of a panel of parents who spoke about their experiences to mental health professionals who work with deaf patients. It was interesting for me to meet with other parents and hear their stories, particularly from parents with children older than my deaf preschooler.

I also had the pleasure to hear the keynote speech by Dr. Gerard Kysela, a professor in education psychology at the University of Alberta, who stated that a developmental view, rather than a disability view, would benefit a deaf child and his or her family the most. We had come to this conclusion as well.

Dr. Kysela's keynote presentation was entitled "How Families Cope with Deafness: A Family Adaptation Model." According to his research, families that have good coping skills and receive support acquire a new set of beliefs and values and adapt well to having a deaf (or disabled) child. He insisted that moving from the pathological (medical) view of deafness to an educational (developmental) view will lead families to concentrate on what the child can do rather than on what he or she can't do.

He said when professionals intervene, the intervention must be family-centered as opposed to the long-held practice of focusing on the child with the disability. Dr. Kysela recommended that parents "reframe the disability and contain the concept of disability to bring it into perspective."

Dr. Kysela advocated a bilingual (ASL and English) approach for language acquisition, as this method can best replicate the ten to twenty million utterances between a "normal" hearing child and a hearing parent, which researchers say is an average exchange over an eighteen- to twenty-month period. Also, he said the family's exposure to Deaf role models is important in their adjustment and the reframing of the disability.

I wrote an article about Dr. Kysela and the conference for the Ontario Medical Association's magazine, which appeared in the July 1995 issue. I am grateful to Jeff Henry, an assistant editor at the time and someone who befriended me when I started working at the OMA, for getting the article included in the issue that went out to all the physicians in the province of Ontario. The article's key message was that physicians, audiologists, and people who service the Deaf community need to view deafness from more than just a pathological viewpoint and to present all the options to families of newly diagnosed deaf or hard of hearing children.

Deaf Babysitters

Two years before attending that conference, Brenda and I were already in the process of reframing the disability and adjusting our perceptive. We were looking at what we could do to adjust to Miranda, rather trying to have her "change" for us. The key was getting to know more deaf people.

Some wise old soul, I'm not sure who, suggested that we hire a Deaf teenager to serve as our babysitter. This was one of the best things we did in the first few months after learning of Miranda's deafness. A deaf babysitter served three purposes for us: (1) we got a care giver who spoke our child's natural language fluently, (2) we got an idea of our child's potential from this deaf adolescent, and (3) Brenda got time to grow her piano-teaching business.

As it happened, Brenda had a friend from church named Paula Buckingham, who was a teacher's aide at the nearest high school, Danforth Technical Collegiate Institute, which had a Deaf students' program. Paula posted a help-wanted notice at the school as a favor to us and also encouraged a couple of girls to consider applying for the job. One of these teenage girls was named Hao Wen Kong.

Hao Wen remembers, "I called Brenda through the relay service. I can't remember what we talked about exactly. I do remember saying a few things about how I could teach Miranda and her parents sign language and Deaf culture. I had no experience with little children. I was a little mortified of making mistakes."

Hao Wen wanted the three-afternoons-a-week job, but because of her class schedule and extracurricular activities could only work two days a week. So she asked a classmate named Jodie to job share. We agreed to hire the girls under this arrangement. Brenda also agreed to pick them up after school and bring them over to our house to babysit for a few hours at a time so she could teach piano, run errands, and enjoy a few moments of freedom from the two kids.

One pleasant spring afternoon, when I arrived home from work, I was introduced to Hao Wen. She was an Asian girl with cute freckles decorating her cheeks, long dark hair, and an outgoing personality with a wonderful sense of humor. A few days later, I met Jodie, an African American girl, who was shy and sweet. Jodie smiled and nodded a lot. At first, we were only able to communicate with the girls writing in a notebook back and forth.

Hao Wen's enthusiasm was great. In time, when her schedule permitted, she became our permanent regular babysitter/nanny. As we got more proficient in signing, we learned more about her. She was a delightful person who was very popular in school, even with the hearing students. In fact, her boyfriend, Glendon, was hearing. They made a sweet couple. According to Hao Wen, he learned to sign nearly fluently in a matter of weeks.

Hao Wen's Story

When Hao Wen Kong was born in Guangzhou, China, in 1974, she had two hearing parents and two hearing brothers. Later, another hearing daughter named Helen was born. Hao Wen is very close to her younger sister. Because Helen is the only one who knows ASL, she serves the role of family interpreter. As Hao Wen recalled:

> My deafness was caused by unknown reasons. My mother took me to several doctors. They said I would be able to hear if I took herbal medicines and had operations. The last doctor we saw told her that I would never hear again. My mother finally accepted that I am officially deaf.
>
> We moved to Canada where my father and grandmother lived in 1980. Deaf education in Canada was valuable to me because the deaf schools in China were more expensive than the public schools [which my family could not afford].
>
> In the fall of 1980, I was placed with an oral class at the Metro Toronto School for the Deaf. I had zero knowledge of letters, words, and numbers. It was frustrating to learn how to speak. Finally, in the fall of 1983, I was placed with a different class of children who knew sign language. I did not know more than twenty or thirty words because I was forced to learn to speak all the time without [learning] what the words mean during oral classes in the past.
>
> I cried all the time because I was so frustrated and overwhelmed with advanced math, vocabulary, and grammar. I tried to communicate so hard with my classmates. It was a few weeks before they accepted me into their groups. Sign language unlocked my communicative barrier and pressures, and I learned so much from educational conversations.

Hao Wen went on to earn a bachelor of fine arts degree in illustration from the Rochester Institute of Technology in Rochester, New York. Now, she works as a CAD (computer-aided design) designer for the family business. She recently married her college sweetheart, Steven Glass, who is a deaf man from Alabama. We stay in contact with Hao Wen via e-mail and still see her on occasion.

Hao Wen's First Day Babysitting Miranda

Hao Wen also recollected the first day of being our babysitter and what our daughter Miranda was like when she first met her:

> When Brenda picked me up after school, I was kind of nervous. She knew almost no sign language. When we arrived at her house, we wrote to each other; however Brenda was anxious to learn and preferred to communicate with me through sign language. She was so eager to learn more from me about the different methods of sign language, ASL, PSE, and SEE, and Deaf culture.
>
> I noticed that Miranda ran around and rarely looked up. Brenda told me she only made strange noises when she wanted something. I tried to chat with her but she wouldn't look at me. So when she wanted a piece of cheese, I taught her the sign. I told her to sign 'cheese' before I gave her some. That was her first sign: 'cheese.'

Inventing Instant Messaging

Believe it or not, I invented instant messaging. It happened when I bought a second-hand Macintosh computer from my office to go along with the Classic II that I already had at home. I set the two computers up on the same desk. When I turned them on and opened the word processing applications the first few times Hao Wen came over to look after the children I'm sure she thought I was crazy. I communicated with Hao Wen by typing words on one computer screen while she typed on the other, taking turns to look over at each other's screens. Why did I resort to this expensive, high-tech "solution?" I didn't have a lot of confidence in my signing skills and was concerned that we wouldn't be able to communicate effectively. Fortunately, I soon developed enough expressive and receptive skills that my two-Mac electronic instant messaging idea was mothballed. I wonder if all those in the Deaf community using instant messaging realize they owe a small debt of gratitude to *moi*?!

For several years, depending on her schedule, Hao Wen babysat Miranda and Terence. We wanted Terence to know how to communicate with his sister, so it was important for him to be exposed to a deaf signer as well. Hao Wen was quite fond of him, describing Terence as "shy and sweet." Terence liked Hao Wen as well and she became a part of our family. We enjoyed her company so much and we learned a great deal about deafness from our daily contact with her.

We were extraordinarily lucky to have Hao Wen come into our lives when she did, and our luck with finding great Deaf role models would continue after we enrolled Miranda into the Happy Hands preschool at the BRCD.

Chapter Three
Preschool and Deaf Role Models

W E WERE EXCITED AND HAPPY when Miranda was accepted into the Happy Hands preschool at the Bob Rumball Centre for the Deaf (BRCD), located in the North York borough of Toronto, a twenty-minute drive from our home in East York. This special preschool's mission is to provide a signing environment for deaf children and the hearing children of deaf parents.

We had nothing but good experiences with the preschool. The teachers and assistants were attentive and loving to the children. Sylvia Goncz, Beverley Dooley-Campbell, and Kim Reid were the teachers I remember best. One was hearing, one was deaf, and one was deafened. They all signed fluently, and it was inspiring to watch them interact with the twenty or so preschoolers who came five days a week for full days.

Miranda quickly made friends and adored the regimen of playtime, learning time, lunchtime, and naptime. As she turned two and began to communicate, Miranda's personality began to emerge, and what joyful moments we experienced with our little "Chubba." She was learning fast, too. By Hao Wen's account, at two years old, Miranda knew about 100 signs.

We discovered Miranda had very rigid standards about her clothing and was a stickler about rules. And when she finds a look that works for her, she sticks with it. When Miranda dressed up as a cat for Halloween, Brenda applied mascara whiskers to her rosy cheeks before going to pre-

Miranda (two) and Terence (four) on Halloween 1993 in our East York home. She is signing "black" as her brother wears her cat costume.

school. Evidently, the response to the costume and events made an impression on Miranda. For the next six months, she would insist on having cat whiskers (sans costume) applied to her face before departing for the preschool.

I have a fond memory of my daughter's intuitive powers when I showed up unannounced once at naptime. The teachers were startled to see me not so much because I was there hours before the normal pick-up time, and not because my wife was the regular pick-up person, but because moments before I arrived, Miranda had awakened from her nap and signed DADDY repeatedly. One teacher tried to get her to go back to sleep, but she refused. While I was holding a sleepy Miranda, the teacher asked if I had informed Miranda I was coming early to get her. I said I hadn't because I hadn't known I was getting off early. Cue *The Twilight Zone* music and get ready for: My Deaf Daughter the Preschool Psychic!

After being in the preschool for about six months, a report card was issued by teacher Sylvia Goncz. The highlights of it were as follows:

Overall, Miranda's receptive language is exceptional. She fully understands many concepts that are related to her through the use of sign language.... Miranda's expressive language is outstanding.... She freely expresses ideas that are related to past or present events.... [Her] cognitive development is strong. She processes information immediately.... Miranda knows all her colours (red, blue, orange, purple, white, yellow and green), numbers (1–5), weather (snowing, sunny, cloudy, rainy) and clothing.... Miranda interacts successfully with the children in the program. She loves to guide and play with her companions during various activities. Hence, she displays confidence and ease when interacting with children.

Miranda will come to a teacher when she is upset, however, at times when feeling frustrated with other children, she may hit them. Also, Miranda still needs assistance when dressing. Moreover, she is ready to begin toilet training.... Miranda has a wonderful disposition and is well liked by all the staff and children in the program. Her enthusiasm, warmth, and curiosity make her a great addition to our program.

Preschool reports are always and should be extremely positive, but we were relieved that our little girl was doing well in an educational setting. Still, I had some concerns and met with teacher Kim Reid to discuss them. The first thing that concerned me was that Miranda often looked away from me before I finished signing to her. Kim reassured me that two-year-olds' attention spans are short. She suggested I work on keeping eye contact by being more animated when communicating.

My second concern was that Miranda often used only one sign to describe something, usually something that she wants, when two signs might be required to get the message across. For example, if she wanted her black shoes, she might sign only BLACK instead of SHOES or BLACK SHOES. Again, Kim reassured me that it wasn't too unusual for kids to do this. She suggested that instead of going off to check everything that is black, simply ask the child for more information.

I guess the solution to my concerns were fairly obvious and simple in retrospect, but these kinds of issues are consistently confronting a new, hearing parent of a deaf child. I will always appreciate the patience and support Miranda's first teachers provided her and our family.

BRCD

"The Bob Rumball Centre for the Deaf, formerly the Ontario Community Centre for the Deaf, is constructed on 6.182 acres of landscaped property in North York. The Centre was officially opened April 5th, 1979 for a cost of $7.3 million, funded by the Ontario Mission, Government of Ontario Grants, the deaf themselves and donations from Churches, service clubs, corporations charitable foundations and concerned citizens," so reads the BRCD's marketing material.

Another brochure states, "At the Centre, professionally trained, deaf and hearing people work with the deaf community to help open doors to a fuller, more satisfying life." The BRCD serves as a senior housing location for deaf seniors who would not do well in a nursing home or senior facility with hearing people. The BRCD is also a hub for Deaf community activity, which includes the housing of special needs deaf people, sign language classes, religious services for the deaf, and of course, the preschool.

Bob Rumball, a Canadian Football League hero, played for the Ottawa Rough Riders and Toronto Argonauts in the 1950s and 1960s. After his playing days were over, he became a reverend and advocate for the Deaf community. Rumball used his high-profile pro sports connections to assist him. A hearing man who doesn't follow the conventional paths, Rumball is a larger-than-life character who, according to BRCD literature, "has dedicated his life to serving the needs of the deaf." Rumball helped make the complex a reality, and he continues to serve the Deaf community in other ways. Hence, the centre bears his name.

The BRCD has a nondenominational, on-site church designed for deaf worshippers. The funding was provided by National Hockey League founder Conn Smythe in memory of his son, Stafford. In addition to the preschool, the complex has apartments for deaf seniors and multi-handicapped adults, a gymnasium, a bookstore, lounges, classrooms, a kitchen, and a dining room. Harold Ballard, the infamous tight-fisted, former owner of the Toronto Maple Leafs, donated the funds for the construction of the dining room.

My First Sign Language Classes

It was at the BRCD that I began taking my first formal sign language classes. I really enjoyed the teachers who were all deaf adults. My first teacher was named Lorraine. She was in her mid-twenties, tall, blond, and attractive. I wondered often if my daughter would grow up to be like her. Lorraine had a delightful presence and carried herself almost regally. She also had a wonderful sense of humor, something I have found in common with all my sign language instructors since.

In the beginner sign language class, I learned quickly, but it never seemed fast enough. I felt I had to grab it all quickly so that I could start modeling language for my daughter the way hearing parents do for their hearing children. Many of my fellow students were there for fun or were fulfilling some kind of school requirement. One of my favorites was a policewoman who wanted to learn how to better communicate with deaf people she interacted with on the job. I applauded her initiative. I wasn't as enamored with other beginners. I was there to learn and it irked me how many of the students continually disobeyed the instructor's request not to speak.

Invariably, these talkers were people who didn't understand what was being expressed in American Sign Language (ASL), so they would start speaking in class instead of sticking with signing and being quiet. There were many times when I wished I could have bonked a few hearing people's heads, as it's extremely difficult to learn to sign when others are chattering. Thankfully, as I progressed through to the higher class levels, the talkers were weeded out. The advanced students were more serious and respectful to the teacher, their fellow learners, and ultimately, the language.

I had a very positive attitude about learning ASL. I felt that it was a great skill to have, and I had always wanted to learn a second language. My high school French and the smattering of Spanish I picked up from living in San Diego were not impressive to anyone, least of all to me. But I had learned the manual alphabet in the sixth grade and never forgot it. I was proud that my sign language was fairly good compared with my fellow classmates. I wanted to stay near the top. It was obvious to me that the better a signer I was, the better I'd be able to communicate with my daughter. Then as now, this is terribly important to me. It remains a continuous challenge.

Still, I had no illusions about impressing anyone with my ASL skills. I was learning this language late in life, and proficiency seemed a much more realistic goal than fluency. In my head, I analogized that my ability to communicate in ASL would be similar to the way my grandfather Enrico Medugno spoke English. He came to America from Italy as a young man and spoke with a thick accent. I figured I wouldn't ever be a beautiful signer, that I'd have a "thick accent," but at least I would be able to get a message across and understand one without too many requests of REPEAT, PLEASE.

My in-laws Barbara and Warren Paddon and brother-in-law, Ian Paddon, felt it was important enough to drive across town one evening every week to take beginning ASL classes. It's tough for seniors to learn a language. As we all know, there is an ideal window of opportunity for learning languages, and for most of us, it closes down in our late adolescence. Despite this limitation, Miranda's grandparents picked up a few signs that they still remember almost ten years later. And they had a good experience with some deaf people and Deaf culture. They still speak glowingly of their one and only ASL teacher Rodney, who was "quite a character."

Ian took an ASL immersion class at the Canadian Hearing Society, taking off work for one week and dedicating his vacation to it. It was an excellent experience for him, and he retained much of what he learned then. To this day, he is the best signer on my wife's side of the family. Because we did not remain in Canada and do not visit family there more than once or twice a year, the other members of the family lost their initiative to learn ASL or attend classes. This is completely understandable as languages are "lost" when not in use daily. Still, we wish, for Miranda's sake, that more of our family signed with more proficiency.

Brenda's family is quite musical, and during our first Christmas after learning that Miranda was deaf, her Uncle Tom and cousin Andrew sang a song and choreographed signs into their performance. The two-year-old Miranda appreciated it so much that by the third verse, she was signing the chorus with them. (Learning ASL signs for holiday nouns and verbs was a fun family activity. One simply can't sign REINDEER and not be jolly doing it.)

Parent Group Meetings

During this time, Brenda and I helped form a parent support group and held meetings once a month at night in the Happy Hands preschool. We found that other (hearing) parents like us needed a place to discuss all the issues of having a deaf child. Unfortunately, we didn't have a strong enough core of people to keep it going more than six months or so.

We were able to invite a different speaker to each meeting. These speakers provided us all with different perspectives on the issues that concerned us. One speaker was the father of a girl who had one of the first cochlear implants in Canada and was being educated in a mainstream high school. The best speaker we had was our representative to the Ontario Provincial Parliament, the Deaf politician, Gary Malkowski.

Deaf Politician Gary Malkowski

One of the good fortunes of my life was meeting Gary Malkowski, "the Deaf politician." There's no better role model for deaf children than Gary. And there is no better example for parents of how successful their deaf child can be. I would argue that Gary's achievement is the highest of any deaf individual in history, based on degree of difficulty and tenure. He did not win either an Academy Award like Marlee Matlin or the Miss America crown like Heather Whitestone. He did not play major league baseball like William "Dummy" Hoy or Curtis Pride nor did he become an educational leader like I. King Jordan and Robert Davila. However, Gary did convince thousands of hearing people with no real understanding of deafness and Deaf culture to elect him to a major legislative body and served as their representative for five years in a high-profile, "very hearing" environment.

Malkowski's life story is fascinating. I've written two major works about him, the first being a full-fledged, 70,000-word biography called *Deaf Politician: The Gary Malkowski Story* (yet to be published), and the second being a two-act play called *Bigger Dreams* (published by 1st Books Library, now known as AuthorHouse). I became an authority on him after spending years researching his history and interviewing many of the people in his life. My conclusion after all this investigation and close examination is that Gary is truly an amazing person.

Briefly, this is Gary's story: He was born into a working-class family in Hamilton, Ontario, a Canadian steel town on Lake Ontario, not far from Niagara Falls. From humble beginnings, he worked his way through a residential school, and despite low-expectations, eventually graduated from Gallaudet College (later University) with a master's degree in counseling.

If that were the end of Gary's achievements, it would be enough to inspire any deaf student. But Malkowski returned to Canada and became an advocate for the Deaf community, organizing protests and serving on numerous committees. He helped pressure the Ontario provincial government to improve deaf education in the province. His advocacy led to repeated contact with political leaders. One leader in particular became his mentor and was key in Gary's decision to run for office and win a seat in the Ontario Provincial Parliament, representing more than 70,000 hearing people as the Member from York East (a section of metropolitan Toronto) from 1990 to 1995.

I first met Gary in the fall of 1993, about nine months after I learned my daughter Miranda was deaf. At that time, we lived on the same street, Queensdale Avenue, one block apart in East York. As I described in both prologues of *Deaf Politician* and *Bigger Dreams*, one morning, Gary drove up to my house to take Miranda to the BRCD preschool along with his son. When my wife had first told me about the carpooling arrangement, I remembered her saying something about Gary being a politician, but the fact that he was also deaf didn't sink in until I met him.

With only a few months of signing classes under my belt, I had a terrible time trying to understand his signing and fingerspelling that first morning. After numerous tries, I finally figured out that he was asking me: "Isn't it strange to have your Member of Provincial Parliament [MPP], driving your child to school?" Yeah, I had to agree it was an odd situation.

As Gary prepared to drive off, he even offered to give me a lift. I was a bit bewildered. Now, my MPP was offering me a ride. I smiled and declined. As I took the subway into my office, I couldn't stop thinking that I had just met a Deaf politician. It seemed like the punch line to a bad joke. Intrigued, I began to do some research on my neighbor and later accepted his frequent invitations to events in and around the community, where he was making public appearances. I was amazed and impressed with his ability to reach people. In time, we became friends, and he has been a major influence on me, demonstrating how to relate to the Deaf community and be an effective father of a deaf child. Because of Gary, I became an activist and an advocate for deaf children. Gary's leadership and friendship also provoked me to take on Canadian citizenship and become a dual citizen, so I could vote for him in the next provincial election. In fact, I also worked on his re-election campaign, which was an amazing experience. I helped by going door to door and dropping campaign literature in mail boxes. I also did some writing that made it into local newspapers.

When the *Toronto Sun*, a right-wing tabloid, tried to foment opposition to Gary's support services in Parliament by writing some unfair and unbalanced articles, I responded with a letter to the editor that was published on April 30, 1994:

RE: "Flap over deaf MPP" (Sun, April 19) and "Dollar signs" (Sun, April 20)

Your paper has done a great disservice to the deaf community and York East with its partisan attack on the NDP's Gary Malkowski. Implying that Malkowski has too many sign language interpreters and they are over-paid may be a legitimate issue to look into, but it's clear your report was not interested in getting the facts straight on such a complex matter.

The sign language interpreters that are needed by a politician must be highly skilled with years of education and experience. The best command the top dollar, as is true in any profession. Furthermore, sign language interpreters are paid on the same scale that French language interpreters are paid. Malkowski needs five interpreters on his staff because of the demands of his position—he works 12-hour days and weekends—and of the necessity for interpreters to spell each other. One cannot simply sit down and interpret eight hours at a time.

Frequent breaks are needed and much time is need for preparing to interpret. Interpreters in many ways are used like machines and that's obviously a demanding chore for any human being. Therefore, one can easily say full-time interpreting is not the same as most "full-time" jobs. Furthermore, the *Sun*'s cavalier treatment of Malkowski's "special" needs implies that he needs five extra people to do the job of one "normal" MPP, like, say [Conservative critic] Chris Stockwell.

It is a huge injustice to put Malkowski in this light. I know because I live in Malkowski's riding [electoral district] and I have a daughter who is deaf. I have witnessed the incredible amount of time and energy he spends on people in both the York East community and in the Deaf com-

At a 1995 fundraiser for Deaf politician Gary Malkowski, member of Ontario's Provincial Parliament. Left to right: Karen Walker (Gary's wife), Gary Malkowski, Richard Medugno, Brenda Paddon.

munity. Why doesn't the *Sun* report any of this? Malkowski's intelligence, diligence, and grace are attributes that all of us that he represents can be proud of. He's a tremendous role model for my daughter and other deaf children. But there are no clever headlines to a story like that, are there?

Because of my close relationship with Gary, he came to me when he was approached by DawnSignPress, a Deaf-run publishing company, about writing his biography. Gary felt he didn't have the time to write his autobiography, and I was happy to sign on, though I warned him that I'd never written a biography before. He had a lot of confidence I could do it, so he recommended me to DawnSignPress and we signed off on contracts. For the next three or four years, I spent most of my free time researching Gary's life and interviewing people like Bob Rae, the former premier of Ontario, and, of course, writing.

Unfortunately, DawnSignPress decided not to publish the manuscript for reasons I never fully understood. Years later, Gallaudet University Press (GUP), the publisher of this book, also decided not to print *Deaf Politician: The Gary Malkowski Story* after initially expressing interest for their Deaf Lives series. The GUP decision was based on the fear of not being able to market a book about a Canadian to readers in the United States. Canadian publishers have been equally concerned, but I know some day the manuscript will be published in some form or another. Gary's life and achievements are too momentous to not be documented in book form for future generations of both hearing and deaf North Americans.

Despite the disappointment of not seeing the work published, I enjoyed the process and felt like it was the start of my "real" writing career, which made working my "day job" at the Ontario Medical Association (OMA) easier to deal with.

Shame on the Ontario Medical Association

Around this time, in the mid-1990s, I worked for the OMA as a supervisor of support services. In this capacity, I began to lobby for OMA to hire disabled people, particularly deaf workers, since I had become a "signer." I had some limited success with hiring a casual employee (a.k.a. a temp) who was a deaf student (our babysitter Hao Wen Kong). If you thought like I did, that the OMA would have been receptive to this idea, you'd be sadly mistaken. People are people whether they're working for a big corporation or a small nonprofit. We all need to be educated and enlightened. We all need our prejudices exposed and our preconceptions challenged.

I wanted to be an agent of change and progress. So when a position under me became available, I lobbied our human resources office to contact the Canadian Hearing Society (a nonprofit advocacy organization where Gary worked before and after his tenure in the Provincial Parliament) for resumes from unemployed deaf candidates. I actually found a candidate who had more than enough qualifications and appropriate experience for the shipping room position and wanted to interview him, but was shot down by my immediate supervisor when I informed him that the candidate may not have any oral skills.

I contacted the human resources folks and soon was in hot water for complaining about my boss's blatant discrimination. Then I was accused of discriminating against women (a totally unfounded counter-charge).

Now my supervisor was investigating me! Yes, the OMA, a union of physicians in the province of Ontario, was allowing job discrimination against a disabled person to occur and then trying to bury the whistle-blower. I was pretty naive.

I was also intimidated into taking no further action. I needed the job, so I kept quiet. The position was eliminated, so no individual, deaf or otherwise, could be hired. I had committed career suicide as far as the OMA was concerned, but Gary was helpful and supportive. One day, he even came into my office and had a "meeting" with me. It was a nice gesture and made me feel better. I made sure my knuckleheaded boss knew I was meeting with the "Deaf politician" that day. I enjoyed seeing his face when he saw me meeting with a member of the Provincial Parliament.

Years later, my former supervisor got fired for some reason unknown to me, but I'm sure it was for some equally stupid misbehavior. I felt like there was some retribution, though justice delayed does seem to be justice denied. The whole experience was painful but eye-opening. People with disabilities have so many hurdles to contend with already, and then they have to deal with boneheads like my former boss who throw up even more road blocks. Even though it is morally reprehensible and, in fact, criminal, they still seem to get away with it.

My favorite personal memory of Gary Malkowski occurred a few weeks after he lost his re-election bid to the Provincial Parliament and no longer had the use of his team of interpreters. He still had commitments to appear at various events. One such event was a Greek community festival. It was an evening gathering in a large empty parking lot with hundreds of Greek immigrants or descendents of Greek immigrants in attendance. Weeks before, Gary had agreed to give a short speech. He had arranged for an interpreter friend to help him with the appearance; but at the last minute, the interpreter called and cancelled due to illness.

This is where I came in. People who know my sign language skills and are reading this are now starting to laugh. I'm no interpreter, but Gary convinced me to go to the event and voice for him. Interpreters need years of training and experience to do a good job. I knew this and foresaw it as a potential fiasco.

Gary wrote out a little speech and gave it to me. I was instructed to read the speech through a microphone while Gary signed his speech on stage. Things went along fine, until I finished voicing the speech and looked up to see Gary still signing. A real ASL interpreter, no matter how good, does not finish voicing before the signer finishes signing—unless he or she has some kind of phenomenal ESP ability. After the speech, all kinds of people came up to greet Gary. I was sweating bullets doing my best to interpret what they were saying and what he was signing. I was so relieved when Gary finally signaled that it was time to go. On the way back to his car, Gary and I laughed ourselves sick about how bad an interpreter I was. (The big joke was "Everything was Greek to me!") Still, Gary got the job done, fulfilling his commitment to the Greek community in his former constituency.

Since leaving the Ontario Provincial Parliament, Gary has continued to maintain a high profile in deaf and disabled rights advocacy. I have a feeling that once his children are older and the time is right, Canadians and the Deaf community will see Gary Malkowski run for office again. Gary continues to add to his legacy as a Deaf role model and trailblazer, making us all proud to know him. I am forever grateful to him for providing me with a view of the potential of deaf people. Because of Gary, I have "bigger dreams" for Miranda.

Chapter Four
Visiting Deaf Schools

IN A FEW YEARS, Miranda would outgrow the Happy Hands preschool at the Bob Rumball Centre for the Deaf (BRCD), and we needed to make a decision about where she would attend elementary school. Because I am an American and Brenda is a Canadian, we had the flexibility to live in either country. We were willing to pack up and move to the best deaf school on the continent, but I hoped it would be close to my relatives in Southern California or Brenda's family in southern Ontario. Career-wise I was ready to start anew, and Brenda could teach piano anywhere.

We were looking for guidance on finding the best place for Miranda to get an education, so I wrote a letter to a well-respected deaf education specialist, asking for her recommendation. Shortly thereafter, in late November of 1993, she was kind enough to take time out of her busy life and write me back. (The professor gave me permission to print this letter as long as she could remain anonymous.)

Dear Mr. Medugno,

I read your letter with much interest.... I'm impressed by your commitment to your daughter's life although I must say that we would respond the same way if our daughter was deaf.

I am not willing to recommend a particular school to you and your wife. The decision really must be yours. I'm willing to share some thoughts on how I might make a decision about a school, and I hope you will find them useful. The first criteria I would use is how many children will be in your daughter's class. Some classrooms can be too small. I don't agree that lower teacher–child ratios are necessarily better. In classrooms that are too small, I feel there isn't enough peer diversity to give a child a sense of social reality. I have observed a classroom with a team of two teachers and twelve students, and I liked the level of peer activity that went on in that classroom. But this is rare. Teachers and schools tend to want smaller classes, in part because they feel overwhelmed by what you have already observed—the wide range of ability they face in one classroom.

I would observe the classroom your child would be placed in, and watch carefully the quality of interaction between teachers and students. Do the students answer the teachers' questions correctly? Do teachers ask expansive questions, or simply yes-no questions? Do the children seem eager to participate, and when they participate, are their contributions on-target and imaginative? If you are not sure of your ability to understand young children signing, ask the school to provide an interpreter for you and your wife. It is important to listen in on children's dialogue with each other and with their teacher. You can learn a lot. I have observed classes where the teacher controlled all interaction, and children contributed very little, or incorrectly. My sense is that teachers who are underskilled in understanding children control the interaction, and the children seem to sense their communicative possibilities with the teacher are limited. When the students talk among each other, one thing to look for is whether they are expanding beyond what their teacher has said (because they do understand).

I would also visit first-, second- and third-grade classes and look for the same things I mentioned earlier, but with an eye to how they teach reading and writing. In my own research, I have found that deaf and hearing teachers teach about written English in different ways. I do not know which is better or worse, but it seems to me that different styles of teaching about English can be useful to the child. At the very least, I would want my child to work with teachers who are skilled signers as well as deaf teachers. Are all the teachers skilled? Is there a good distribution of hearing and deaf teachers? Are deaf teachers equal participants in the goals of the elementary program?

I think all the schools you mentioned would be on my list if I were looking for one for my daughter. It has to be a tough decision, but you should reassure yourself that your daughter is off to a very good start (the size of her sign vocabulary is about the same as my [hearing] daughter's), and the fact that you are both signing with her will make up for the inevitable deficiencies of any school.

We really appreciated these suggestions and employed many of them while on our school visits.

Visiting Deaf Schools

So Brenda and I researched deaf schools throughout North America. We wanted to find the school that would be best for Miranda. We were willing to move to almost any place. We visited a number of deaf schools in both the United States and Canada. Our evaluating focused on schools that had strong reputations in the Deaf community and adhered to a bilingual-bicultural (bi-bi) philosophy in education.

The first place we checked out was the E. C. Drury School for the Deaf in Milton, Ontario. This was a provincial school where most of the students were residents during the week and went home on the weekend. Milton is a bedroom community of greater Toronto, and many of its residents commute into the big city via the train. We weren't overly impressed with the school, which seemed to be in a struggle over its overall philosophy and in constant fear of governmental interference in its education process or the cutting of funding. Though this was Gary Malkowski's alma mater, we just couldn't see it as one of our top choices.

The Metro Toronto School for the Deaf, where our babysitter Hao Wen Kong attended as a child, has a Total Communication philosophy and shares space with a local elementary school for hearing children. Some of the deaf students were mainstreamed into regular classes; but for the most part, what we saw was that the deaf and hearing kids did not interact much. It seemed to us that Miranda got enough of the deaf and hearing dynamic at home with her parents and brother. We wanted to give her a place where the playing field was level: a place where language wouldn't be an issue, where everyone spoke the same language.

I visited California's two state schools for the deaf in March of 1994. The first stop was the San Francisco Bay area and the city of Fremont, which is southwest of the city and northeast of San Jose. Fremont is considered both a part of Silicon Valley and East Bay. It's a fairly new city of 200,000 souls, making it the fourth-largest populated Bay Area community, trailing only San Jose, San Francisco, and Oakland. However, it does not have a cohesive, city atmosphere and feels like a giant suburb without a heart or hub. Fremont does claim to be "a city with a mission." The historic Mission San Jose sits in the shadow of Mission Peak in the southern section of Fremont. Formed in the late 1950s by combining five towns that are now the city's districts, Fremont is a safe, fairly affluent community, which is a tad on the boring side.

When I drove up Stevenson Boulevard, past Lake Elizabeth and the Central Park playing fields, and prepared to turn onto Gallaudet Drive, the rolling and green East Bay hills served as a majestic backdrop for the California School for the Deaf's (CSDF's) campus. Something in me clicked, and I whispered to myself, "This is it!" I actually got teary-eyed.

Intellectually, I knew both my wife and I would have to tour the school and other institutions and investigate the job market before any final decisions could be made. Emotionally, the decision for me was made the instant I saw the campus.

However, I knew that my intuition wasn't going to be enough to convince Brenda or anyone else that this was the right place for us. So I kept an open mind as the deaf, diminutive, and delightful Hedy Udkovich Stern from the CSDF's outreach department gave me the school tour.

The CSDF has a long history, although it has only been in Fremont since 1980. Prior to that, it was located in Berkeley, near the University of California, Berkeley, campus, for more than 100 years. The decision to move south was due to the school purportedly being situated on an earthquake fault line. I have heard a Deaf community rumor that UC Berkeley coveted the deaf school land and took over the site when the new school opened in Fremont.

Dr. Henry Klopping has been the superintendent of CSDF since before the relocation to Fremont. The hearing son of deaf parents, Hank is a much admired and beloved administrator. I recall reading about him and the school in Oliver Sacks's book *Seeing Voices*. Because of CSDF's extraordinary reputation, it was high on my list of "must-visit" schools. I was not disappointed.

Hedy gave me a welcome kit with all the information a relocating family would need. I took photos of the school because I knew they would help Miranda visually understand when we talked about a "new school in California." Hedy was a good sport and posed next to the famous "Bear Hunt" statue by CSDF alumnus sculptor Douglas Tilden, which stands at the front of the school. We had a good laugh as she played around with different silly poses before she settled on a mature-professional-woman-admiring-a-work-of-art pose.

After seeing the school and driving up into the East Bay hills for a better view of the surroundings, I headed south to San Diego, my hometown, fairly sure that we would be moving to Fremont. We had previously visited the deaf program in San Diego's school district and weren't impressed. So I was eager to check out the California School for the Deaf in Riverside (CSDR). My father and stepmother accompanied me. They were eager for me and my family to move much closer to them than Toronto or the San Francisco Bay area, so they lobbied gently for Riverside.

Unfortunately, having grown up in San Diego, I had a pretty negative opinion of Riverside. The area is nicknamed "the Inland Empire" for some reason. San Diegans like me had our own nickname for Riverside. We called it "the armpit" of Southern California. When I said this to Ethan Bernstein, one of the principals of CSDF's high school and a graduate of CSDR, he laughed. He didn't think it was that bad, and he signed to me, "Well, everyone needs an armpit!"

My visit to CSDR didn't change my opinion of Riverside, though the school wasn't bad. The day we visited, it was eighty degrees outside. I dreaded the idea of being there in the summer, when it is really hot and smoggy. The school buildings were still mostly in the same condition from when the campus was built in the early 1950s, though some were being refurbished. Ultimately, I saw some things I liked about Riverside, but I didn't get the same good vibe I got when I visited Fremont.

The CSDR's outreach department at the time was not very strong. In fact, they forgot I was coming to tour the school that day. About six months later, in the fall of 1994, Brenda, Miranda, and my mother-in-law, Barbara, replicated my trip and had the same experience and got similar impressions. At CSDF, Hedy and Miranda became fast friends, whereas the outreach folks at Riverside forgot that Brenda was coming to tour their campus. I understand CSDR was going through some rough times. I understand things are much better there now. Nevertheless, we pretty much had our sights set on Fremont, though we did continue to investigate other institutions.

In September of 1994, during what will forever be known to us as "the weekend of wetness," Brenda and I packed Miranda and her brother Terence into our car and drove across New York and Massachusetts to Boston for my Auntie Sue's seventieth birthday party and to check out the Learning Center. It was the "weekend of wetness" because it rained the entire trip to Boston, the entire time we were there, and the whole way back to Toronto. And if it wasn't wet enough outside, our five-year-old and three-year-old were

Three-year-old Miranda with grandmother Barbara Paddon visiting the California School for the Deaf–Fremont campus for the first time. The statue by famous CSD alumnus Douglas Tilden is called The Bear Hunt.

wetting the inside of the car. We briefly considered putting them both back in diapers, because it was getting ridiculous.

The Learning Center was nice and quaint, but small. At the time, I believe they only had about 250 students, which was half the attendance of the Fremont school. Having lived in the Boston area for two years, I knew the school was going to have to meet all our criteria to justify me moving back to New England. I love all my Irish and Italian relatives and visiting Boston, but I hated living there for those two years. Though born in Ft. Benning, Georgia, as an army brat, I was raised in San Diego County and am a California boy at heart.

Another school that I had heard many good things about was the Maryland School for the Deaf (MSD), where Gary Malkowski's old classmate, James Tucker, was the superintendent. I wanted to visit MSD before we made our final decision. The opportunity came in June of 1995 when Tucker asked Gary to give the commencement address at the graduation ceremony. I accompanied Gary down to Maryland the day after he lost his re-election bid in Ontario. I expected Gary to be upset and depressed as we drove down from Toronto, but in fact, he was surprisingly upbeat. While there, we shared a dorm room on the MSD campus. At last, a roommate who wouldn't be bothered by my snoring.

I found MSD, located in Fredrick, Maryland, to be an impressive school. It had some key advantages—one being its close proximity to Washington, D.C., and Gallaudet University. James Tucker was very warm and friendly with me. He lobbied me to consider moving to Maryland so Miranda could attend school there. He was persuasive and I appreciated being wooed, but I really thought we would be better off in California, all things being equal with the schools.

This weekend trip with Gary was one of Deaf immersion. As I sat at a table in a Frederick restaurant with Gary and James, I got a real sense of what it must be like to be a deaf person surrounded by hearing people. It is not terribly pleasant. James, who is technically hard of hearing and has a good speaking voice, reminded me of this when Gary left us alone for a few minutes. James asked me if I was following their conversations. I said I was struggling, but I thought I was getting the gist most of the time. He said, "I'm glad you are having this experience because this is what it's like for your daughter in the hearing world." It was a lesson I appreciated.

Reading *Deaf in America,* Meeting Author Carol Padden

One of the first books I read during that first year following the discovery that Miranda was deaf was *Deaf in America: Voices from a Culture* by Carol Padden and her husband Tom Humphries. It was fascinating reading about the history and culture of the deaf, which I had no idea existed. As it happens, Padden and Humphries were professors at the University of California, San Diego (UCSD), and, as most of my family still resides in San Diego, I put contacting these Deaf authors the next time I visited home on my to-do list.

In addition to residing in my hometown, there was another coincidence: the resemblance between my wife's last name and Carol's—Paddon vs. Padden. I thought they might be distantly related, but as it turned out, Carol's ancestry is from Russia and her immigrant forefathers changed their last name upon arriving in the New World, whereas Brenda's family heritage is from the British Isles.

When I wrote Carol, she wrote back saying she would be happy to meet with me. So the next time I traveled to Southern California, I met with Dr. Padden at her office on the UCSD campus in La Jolla. Because of some unexpected duties that required her immediate attention, she only had a few minutes for me. Carol is deaf but has a good speaking voice. She seems to straddle the Deaf and hearing cultures with aplomb, though the Deaf community is clearly her "home."

I enjoyed conversing with Dr. Padden and really appreciated her willingness to chat with a hearing parent. I asked Carol a few specific questions about deaf education and Deaf culture. There wasn't time to answer them in the depth that she would have liked, so she asked me to meet her and her three-year-old daughter Jacy for dinner at a restaurant in Del Mar that evening.

I don't recall what Carol and I discussed at the restaurant, but I enjoyed the meal and had fun teasing Jacy, which made me homesick for my own little girl back in Canada. I told Carol about my recent visit to Fremont and how I thought it was the best school I'd seen so far. Carol saw the benefits of a number of institutions but supported my view that the California School for the Deaf in Fremont was one of the better schools in the country.

Chapter Five
Hearing Brother, Deaf Sister

BEING THE SIBLING OF A DEAF BROTHER or sister is not easy. There are many issues besides the normal sibling rivalries. The biggest one is, of course, communication. As our son Terence began to go to school, it became apparent that we were going to have to work hard at getting him to communicate with his sister Miranda in her natural language. Quite naturally, he resisted having to use his eyes and hands to communicate when he recently mastered the art of conversing with ears and mouth.

Sometimes I forget he was there from the start, too. Oh, he may have only been three-and-a-half years old when we learned that his sister was profoundly deaf, but he did understand the problem. "Miranda's ears are broke," he said. Of course, he didn't understand the ramifications then. Maybe he thought she would "get better" or that his mother or I could "fix" her like we could one of his broken toys. Maybe he didn't understand that we didn't think she was broken or needed to be fixed.

However, years later, when Terence understood the ramifications of his sister's deafness, he certainly didn't appreciate them. His sister was different from his friends' sisters. His sister couldn't talk. His sister couldn't hear. His sister wanted him to interpret things for her. It's not fair! He had to learn sign language. He had to look at her or get her to look at him to communicate. When she covered her eyes to avoid receiving his thoughts, threats or theories, he got really frustrated. It's not fair!

Then there were the things that happen in public. When his sister made funny noises or did the wrong thing, and people stared. It embarrassed him, especially when she visited his school.

Oh, sure, we told him how lucky he was to have a beautiful, loving sister who opened a whole new world to us all. "She is a blessing that we cherish and are proud of." He didn't buy it, at least not

Two-year-old Miranda's birthday party with Terence and Brenda in our East York home in 1993.

then. All he saw was Miranda getting much more attention than he did. He saw all the extra efforts made to accommodate her. Then he experienced his sister and her friends making fun of him and the way he signed. This is not the way it should be, he must have thought.

"It's not fair!" he said.

"Life's not fair," I told him. It didn't help. I sometimes wish that we had a deaf child first. It seems that when the older child is deaf, the younger one learns to sign easier and have a better relationship because the younger one wants to emulate the older one. It seems even better if the siblings are the same sex. They have more in common then—or so it seems. But all this wishful thinking doesn't change anything.

I learned that the more I pushed my son into improving his relationship with his sister, improving his signing skills, and accepting her the way she is, the more he resisted. He would have to come to terms in his own good time—as painful and sad as it was to witness and experience.

There are heartbreaking times when brother and sister are so frustrated and angry with each other—unable or unwilling to communicate on a basic level. But then there are other moments when they are communicating and enjoying each other's company. It is heartwarming and inspiring to see these moments. My fondest hope is that some day they will eventually have a close-knit relationship and will be supportive and proud of each other without reservations. I hope some day that they will realize how much they need each other. How can I help them understand the importance of this? I honestly don't know. Does anyone know how to bridge siblings so there's revelry and not rivalry? I have ideas and hopes and dreams—but no guarantees. And that scares me sometimes.

Communication Methods
in a Blended Hearing Deaf Family

Brenda and I work hard to keep Miranda in the loop when we are talking with Terence and other hearing people with whom we have contact. We do not sign all the time in her presence. I know that Deaf culture considers this incredibly rude. However, when hearing parents learn American Sign Language (ASL) late in life, they will find it nearly impossible to sign ASL and speak English at the same time. We still usually start conversations using both languages, but invariably drop one or the other, depending on the situation, and go exclusively with the language that is most appropriate at the time.

Just as we feel Miranda has a right to communicate in her natural language, we feel that Terence has a right to communicate in his, especially when he is not talking to his sister. A mother with a younger deaf daughter and an older hearing son, like our family makeup, told me how upset her son got when she asked him to sign when he was trying to tell her about something exciting that happened at school. The boy was only seven or eight and didn't know all the signs for what he wanted to tell his mother, and he broke down in tears of frustration. I wonder if forcing a hearing child to always use ASL will lead to deep resentment and ultimately be counterproductive.

Another family with a hearing daughter a few years younger than their deaf son, told me that when she is talking excitedly about something in her life that she wants to share with them and she's asked to sign, she will just close down and say, "Never mind." The difficulty of expressing herself naturally in her second language undercuts her desire to communicate.

Some might say that if children use their second language enough, they'll be fluent in both. Nice idea in theory, but everyone's different, and life is not a perfectly controlled environment. I think emotions need to be vented naturally, and we have to allow our hearing children that right.

In our house, we interact with our children in their mother tongue (or thumb), and then interpret soon thereafter for the other child, if he or she is present during the interaction. It remains a challenge, and perhaps I am rationalizing our method. I am sure we could do better. I suspect Miranda, as she becomes older, will help us make things more accessible for her. I want her to be able to demand for herself what she needs.

Silent Voice Summer Program Scare

In the summer of 1994, when Terence turned five years old, Brenda and I enrolled him in the Sign Language Summer Program (SLSP) day camp run by the Silent Voice organization. Miranda was too young for the program and continued to go to the Happy Hands preschool at the Bob Rumball Centre for the Deaf (BRCD). The objectives of the SLSP, according to documentation we received were five-fold:

- To provide a summer sign language day camp for deaf children and for hearing children who have a deaf family member
- To teach independence in various life skills
- To provide children with a range of community life experiences
- To introduce children to Deaf adult role models
- To teach cooperation in a deaf-hearing mixed group

As the counselors were all deaf adults, this program would be a "total immersion" for Terence for five or six hours a day. We were fairly confident that this day camp would help Terence acquire more ASL and quickly. Unfortunately, this was not a successful venture and nearly proved to be disastrous.

In theory, this program would have been good for some five-year-olds, but Terence was on the young side and tended to be a bit introverted. After just a few days, Brenda felt that Terence was not fitting in well, and she had some concerns about the way the program was being run. It was not structured well, nor was it supervised adequately from her point of view. For example, because there weren't enough counselors, some of the young children were sent to the rest rooms with slightly older kids as escorts.

One summer day when I got home from work, my wife and kids weren't there, and the light was blinking on our answering machine. I listened to a message that concerned me greatly. The director of the SLSP day camp called to "apologize for what happened today." Of course, I thought, "What the hell happened?!" A short time later, our babysitter Hao Wen Kong called via relay, asking whether Brenda had found Terence yet. "WHAT?!" was my response.

I soon learned that the summer program had taken the kids to the Metro Toronto Zoo and mistakenly left my five-year-old son there. The counselors didn't even know Terence was missing until they arrived back at the school. Brenda was waiting there, and when our son didn't appear from any of the three returning buses, she tried not to panic.

Brenda had been apprehensive about the field trip all day. The program had displayed a "loose" organizational style in the first week, which had us both wondering whether we should continue to send Terence there.

Now, in the second week, we had a frightening confirmation. Brenda did not let her concern override her reason. Despite a sluggish response by the counselors to the question "Where is my son?"—she avoided wringing their necks. She found a phone, called the zoo, and got through voicemail hell to the administrative personnel, who assured her there were no lost children there. Then she was connected to the nurse's office, where they did have a lost little boy.

Brenda was relieved to hear Terence's little voice when the nurse put him on the line. We don't know how long Terence was on his own. It chilled me to the bone to even think about him being lost in such a huge public place. To think about what could have happened is self-torture.

According to Terence, a woman found him crying and asked what was wrong. He said, "I lost my group." The woman did what most of us would do, and for which we were extremely grateful: She took Terence to a zoo representative.

Brenda had a long drive to the Metro Toronto Zoo, fighting traffic and fuming about the violation of our trust by the day camp program.

She didn't have time to notify me of all that had occurred, so I didn't hear all the details until they had arrived home. Terence didn't seem to be at all traumatized. Brenda chalked it up to his being naive and having faith that wherever he was, she'd find him. He was still at an age where he thought his parents were superheroes. For example, my super power was that I "know everything." It was hard to argue with him about that.

Our concern and reaction must have crept into Terence's subconscious. A couple of nights later, he woke up from a bad dream. He dreamt he was at a swimming pool with the summer program and the counselors threw him into the deep end. He was struggling to swim and keep his head above water. Symbolically, I think this is a pretty good representation of what had really happened.

We sent a letter to the executive director of Silent Voice, Beverly Pageau, expressing our huge disappointment and asking her to scrutinize the elements of the program before someone else's child suffered the same or a worse fate. She responded with a letter of her own, apologizing profusely and assuring us that they would take our suggestions and fix all the problems with the SLSP. Needless to say, we withdrew Terence from the day camp. I'm sure Terence would put this experience, along with having to move to California, at the top of his list of "Why It Ain't Easy to Have a Deaf Sibling."

We didn't want someone at the program to be made a scapegoat and fired due to inadequate management. It seemed to us that the counselors were not properly selected, trained, or supervised, and the blame should fall on the management of the program.

I still don't understand why the counselors in question didn't do a simple head count before leaving the zoo. Terence may not have been the most memorable or vocal of children, but there weren't many five-year-olds with glasses at the day camp. You would have thought the counselor responsible for him would have wondered long before the buses arrived back in East York, "Hey, where's the kid with glasses?"

Ironically, the parent's manual given to us by the SLSP states, "During our weekly trips, the most important consideration is the safety of the children." Clearly, this was an inexcusable error by an individual and an organization that seemed to have no appropriate system in place, despite professing that their utmost concern was safety.

Nearly ten years later, it is still upsetting to think that this happened. Silent Voice had been such a godsend when we first found out Miranda was deaf, but unfortunately this incident forever tarnished our appreciation of the agency.

This experience also unfortunately undermined some of my trust in Deaf community for a time. At this point, I actually had not known very many Deaf adults. Though the negligent counselor was identified and punished, I couldn't help feeling that a mature, intelligent person would never have been guilty of such a mistake. Were all Deaf people like this? Intellectually, of course, I knew this was not true; but emotionally, it took some time to get over the stereotype I was formulating. It helped knowing that both our close Deaf friends, Hao Wen and Gary Malkowski, were equally outraged by the incident.

I squirm a little when I wonder what would have happened had Miranda ever been left behind in such a place. It is one of the scariest things about having a young deaf child. The fear of losing Miranda in a department store or amusement park and her not being able to hear me call her name was a nightmare that kept me hyper-vigilant. I never took my eye off her in those situations. When we visited large places with lots of people, we made contingency plans; if she were to lose track of us, she was told to go to a certain place and wait. It is always a concern for parents of all children, but more so for parents of deaf children.

Miranda's biggest scare as a young child was when she got locked in my in-laws' basement bathroom. She was around three years old, and when she couldn't turn the lock on the door handle, she began banging on the door and crying. When the adults got there and began to fiddle with the knob from the outside, she began to panic. We guessed she realized that we could not open the door either. It was heartbreaking not being able to reassure her with our voices. So while my father-in-law got his toolbox to dismantle the knob, on a piece of paper, I quickly sketched a scene of her behind the door and us on the other side trying to help. I slid it under the door to a preliterate Miranda, hoping she would understand we were working on freeing her. It did calm her some. A visibly shaken little girl emerged from the bathroom a few minutes later. From then on, we made sure that Miranda knew how to unlock doors after that experience.

Local TV News Appearance

After the final decision had been made in early 1996 and a couple of months before we planned to relocate to California, we were recommended by teachers at the Happy Hands preschool to be interviewed for a TV news program. We were contacted by a producer for the news department on the Global TV network, a major independent network in Canada, to be interviewed for a story they were doing on cochlear implants. At the time, implants represented a hugely controversial issue between the Deaf and medical communities. It seems less so now, at least in the United States, where the government doesn't pay for the procedure.

I believe the news producer saw Brenda and me as representatives of the "crazy fringe" of hearing parents who didn't want to "cure" their child with cochlear implant surgery. We did our best to explain to her why we didn't think it was necessary and that we didn't believe the procedure was a true cure for the condition of deafness. I believe it is a fair analogy to say that an implant gives the deaf "hearing" the way a wheelchair gives paraplegics "mobility." A cure is not something that can break down or has numerous limitations.

The producer interviewed another family who had chosen to have their two-year-old implanted. I gathered from their profile that they knew next to nothing about the Deaf community and seemed to have very little interest in learning. I worried that they had high expectations that the child would be "normal" after the operation. The news people further blurred the line by comparing the child with an older man who lost his hearing late in life and then gotten an implant. They showed a scene of the man saying to the uncomprehending two-year-old, "You're just like me." Sorry, sir, that's just not true. The old man and the child are in very different situations.

If the news folks were interested in really doing an informative story about cochlear implants, they should have been interviewing families with older children and then contrasted and compared the differences between a deaf kid, unaided in a deaf school, and an implanted kid in a mainstreamed (hearing) school.

Yes, cochlear implants have been very successful for people who have been deafened late in life. And it's even assisted prelingually and profoundly

Four-year-old Miranda enjoys graduation day from the BRCD preschool in June 1996 with father, mother, and brother Terence.

deaf children to acquire speech. However, you still have a child who has "major hearing issues." From a strictly hearing person's perspective, one may think the more hearing, the better. This is a bias that ignores the fact that in many cases, "less is more." At their best, cochlear implants make deaf people like hard of hearing people, who often complain bitterly of being stuck between the Deaf and hearing worlds.

This is a complicated issue. Unfortunately, television news is about sound bites and visuals, and they lead to very superficial treatment and understanding of any complicated issue. Because of the way our interview was edited, I felt we were presented "as well meaning but naive" parents. Perhaps, many labeled us "Luddites" or "technophobes" who should just jump on board the implant express. Sorry folks; TRAIN GO SORRY. (This is an idiom used in the North American Deaf community that means, "Sorry, you missed the boat.")

We'd seen so many successful deaf people who didn't even need hearing aids in their lives, much less an implant, it was relatively easy for us to decide that this technology was not appropriate for our child. However, if she chooses to have an implant later in life, we will support her decision.

Our decision to let Miranda decide if and when she wants a cochlear implant seemed the best option. Granted, she may miss the optimum time to learn speech if she chooses to wait to have the operation; but almost assuredly, the procedure will be less risky in the future and the technology will be more sophisticated. I remain comfortable with that decision today, nearly a decade later. At this point, Miranda has expressed no desire to be implanted.

In the future, I will think long and hard about volunteering again to be interviewed by TV journalists. If I were in that situation again, I would do a better job of staying on message. However, the risk remains that your quotes will be taken out of context and be used to undermine your position. That's the chance you take when dealing with the media.

Going Away Party

When our lease expired in April 1996, we moved out of the home we had been renting in East York and moved in with my in-laws for a few months. Their house was located west of Toronto in the city of Mississauga. I continued to work until the end of June, so we could save on a few months' rent. Consequently, the whole family commuted into Toronto for two months. Driving in the morning rush on the Queen Elizabeth Expressway was not much fun. So when my last day of work arrived, it felt so much like someone had presented me with a "Get of Jail Free" card. After nine years of working with the same company, the last five serving under a knucklehead boss, I basically skipped out of the Ontario Medical Association office and never looked back. I had stayed too long, but now I was free. Soon, I would be leaving Canada after nine long, eventful years and heading home to America. It felt good.

On the weekend before we left, my in-laws Barbara and Warren had a little going-away party for the family. As easy as it was to say *sayonara* to my job, it was as hard to say goodbye to the people who had supported and loved us so much in Ontario. We wouldn't really know how much we appreciated family and friends, until we moved to Fremont where there were neither.

Chapter Six
"California Here We Come..."

MIRANDA WAS A STUDENT at the Happy Hands Preschool at the Bob Rumball Centre for the Deaf (BRCD) for nearly three years before we left Canada for northern California so she could attend the renowned California School for the Deaf (CSDF) in the city of Fremont on the southeast edge of the San Francisco Bay.

Moving to Fremont without family, friends, or jobs lined up was a huge leap of faith. Fortunately, in the summer of 1996, Silicon Valley was ramping up for the boom of the "dot-com" era, so I suspected I'd be able to find work pretty quickly, but still it was scary. My appreciation grew for the pioneers and forty-niners who came to California 150 years earlier. It was hard enough for us even with all the modern conveniences.

Fortunately, we had some savings to cushion us for a few months. However, it was painful to exchange our Canadian dollars for U.S. ones. The exchange rate was about 65 percent, if I recall correctly. We shipped most of household items, but we had to buy a car and major pieces of furniture. And we had to find a place to live.

The plan was for us to fly into San Diego, visit family, purchase a vehicle, and drive up the coast. I had made arrangements with the always-helpful CSDF representative Hedy Udkovich Stern to stay on the school campus in one of the parents' visiting apartments for a week or two, until we found our own place.

Buying a Car

I didn't realize how stressful it was going to be to buy a car with only a few days to shop. Fortunately, my father was able to assist in carting me around San Diego. One memorable stop on the mission involved a "curbsider." I responded to an ad and agreed to meet the man in a shopping plaza where the car for sale was parked.

I don't know what it was about the guy, but during our test-drive, my internal "bullshit detector" was going off like a fire alarm in my head. Of course, that's not surprising anytime you are dealing with someone who is trying to sell you a used car. This character was just a little too slick. I didn't say much while he chatted up my father. Then he began to tell us a story about a car that his friend wanted to sell, which had a really bad knocking engine. He said, "So my friend said, 'Nobody is going to buy this car.' I told him, 'Oh, yeah, someone will. Just sell it to a deaf guy!' Hahahahaha."

If he hadn't been wearing his seatbelt, I would have been tempted to hit the brakes and send this idiot flying through the windshield. I burned slowly inside but said nothing. I drove the car back to the shopping plaza and said, "Thanks but no thanks." When we were alone, my father asked me why I didn't like the car. I said, "Doesn't matter, Dad. I would never do business with an asshole like that."

"But if you like the car and the price, forget about what he said," said my father.

"No way." Later, I found out more about curbsiders that I should have known. Many like to hoodwink buyers with cars that won't pass inspection; and once you've paid your money, they are long gone.

The next day, I bought a used Nissan Sentra from a car dealer. It was exactly the kind of car I was looking for. Soon the stress of car shopping melted away, and finally I could relax a little and enjoy visiting San Diego and my family.

Communicating with Relatives

I come from a large Italian-Irish Catholic family, based in San Diego. Holiday visits with my extended family had always been stressful because there are always lots of people around, and in our efforts to include Miranda and make events more accessible, we felt we could not relax.

When she was just a two-year-old, Miranda gave us quite a scare in San Diego, escaping the confines of my father's gateless backyard. Our toddler toddled down the sidewalk next to a busy street and ended up in the complex nearby, knocking on apartment doors. It was a harrowing few minutes between learning that Miranda wasn't in the house or the backyard until we found her. The futility of yelling out your deaf child's name certainly can be frustrating and add to your anxiety level during moments like these. Thankfully, Miranda's disappearances did not happen very often. Her escape did provoke my father to hire a contractor to build gates for his yard the next day.

One of the downsides of the choice to live in Fremont, so far from family, is that no relatives have been able to learn or retain enough sign language to communicate freely with Miranda. Some recall a few basic signs and some can fingerspell. Mostly they rely on gesturing, note-writing, or Brenda, Terence, and me facilitating communication between Miranda and themselves.

Two of my sisters actually hired sign language instructors to come to their homes for private lessons with their kids. However, since one sister lives in San Diego and the other in Portland, the interaction between cousins isn't frequent enough to support the acquisition of the new language. Still, we appreciated the efforts. I suspect that down the road, thanks to the early exposure, my nieces and nephews will learn and retain American Sign Language (ASL) in a high school or community college class. At least that is one of my hopes.

Miranda has three girl cousins who are about the same age. Emily is the oldest by a year, Miranda and Hannah were born on the same day of the same year, and Nicole was born a week later. They do not get the chance to visit together very often. The first time was when they were two-year-olds and all could barely talk, except for Emily who was a sophisticated conversationalist from an extremely early age. At that time, the girls got along fine.

After our move, at the age of five, Miranda's deafness set her apart from her cousins, and she was frequently excluded from play. This, of course, was predictable but extremely painful to watch. In retrospect, I wish I had not just sat back and let it happen so often. Unfortunately, it wasn't until years later, after some trial and error and brainstorming, that was I able to come up with a long list of activities that deaf and hearing kids can play together successfully. (See the appendix at the end of this book.) In this kind of situation, the parents need to be the initial facilitators and should spend a lot of time with the kids to make it happen successfully.

Brenda did step in often. One memorable time was when she had Miranda and a cousin alone in a hotel swimming pool. Miranda wanted to interact with her cousin who refused to play and repeatedly splashed water in Miranda's face. Just in case you had any doubts, splashing a deaf kid in the eyes is really uncool. This was so hurtful to our daughter.

Brenda took the cousin aside and explained that Miranda has feelings and is a real person even if she doesn't know how to talk. Of course, the cousin was far too young to really understand the ramifications of her behavior, and she was not a mean child. She just had this cousin whom she couldn't communicate with, and that was frustrating her so she didn't want any part of it.

As parents, we probably could have saved our daughter and her cousin this painful interaction, which, of course, seven years later, neither remembers, if we had facilitated more. Brenda and I recall this so clearly because it is devastating to see your child ostracized right before your eyes.

In retrospect, I know my sister was disappointed in her daughter because she had spent time preparing her to be with Miranda. But kids are kids and they all learn lessons. We all got over it, although, not surprisingly, Miranda is still an outsider when all the cousins are all together.

Another unpleasant memory occurred when Miranda was about eight or nine years old and we were visiting San Diego. We made plans to go to our family's favorite pizza place, Filippi's Restaurant in Pacific Beach. My sister Michele let her daughter Emily invite a friend to join us, not realizing the ramifications. Emily sat between her friend and Miranda and spent the entire time in the restaurant, quite naturally, focused on her friend while Miranda was left out. The adults were involved in having a good time, eating and chatting. At some point, I looked at Miranda and she signed to me "I feel lonely."

It was like someone stabbed a knife into my heart. I signed, "I'm sorry" and burst into tears. It hurt so much to see my little girl feeling isolated and alone while surrounded by my family who love her dearly. Needless to say, my becoming emotional about the situation put a damper on the evening, but I think we all learned from the experience. We had to be more proactive.

Now, we try to avoid these situations, if at all possible. One successful way to address it is to have Miranda invite a deaf friend to come along so she has someone with whom to communicate when the hearing girls want to chatter. This seemed to work quite well. Two deaf girls signing to one another turns heads and seems more interesting and cool to the hearing kids, as opposed to a single deaf girl trying to interact with her hearing peers. I am not sure why this is. If I hazard a guess, I'd say it is because one is an "oddity" and two is the start of a team with its own secret code, which other kids may want to join.

Fourth of July on the Beach

While we were on the beach in San Diego that Fourth of July in 1996 celebrating with our family, a deaf man selling balloons, flags, and other patriotic paraphernalia approached us when he saw us signing to Miranda. He introduced himself and we started conversing with him. We told him how we had just moved to California and our daughter was going to go to school in Fremont. He brightened and said that his daughter attended the CSDF. After he departed, Brenda and I looked over to see our family all staring at us. They'd never seen us carry on an adult conversation in ASL. They had only seen us communicating with Miranda. They were very impressed with us. It was then that I realized this is something to be proud of. I can communicate in more than one language now. Finally.

Heading North

A few days later, we headed north for Fremont. The drive was uneventful. We arrived at the CSDF campus and settled into our temporary quarters with a heavy sigh of relief. As school was not in session, the campus was deserted and a little too quiet, especially at night. We couldn't wait to get out and start our new lives: meeting people, finding a place to live, finding livelihoods, and becoming rooted in the community. Maybe because we were so anxious, all these things took a lot longer to become a reality than we had anticipated.

This school accommodation saved us hundreds of dollars in hotel bills. This support made our transition a great deal less stressful. It wasn't an easy chore finding an apartment that was available immediately, in a reasonable price range, and close to the school.

We also had to prove we had an income, although Brenda and I didn't have jobs yet. That took some imagination, but we worked it out. I informed the apartment management that I was a freelance writer and showed them a copy of the book contract I had with DawnSignPress for the Malkowski biography, which ultimately did not get published. I have some residual bitterness about that, but at least DSP, in a way, helped me get into a home. The contract seemed to impress the manager enough to qualify us for an apartment.

We moved into our new place in Crossroads Village a week or so after arriving in Fremont. The apartment complex was ideally situated in a central part of the city, within walking distance to a shopping center, Lake Elizabeth, the library, and a grocery store. Terence's school, W.W. Brier Elementary, was a block west, while Miranda's new school was about a mile east.

We rented a two-bedroom, first-floor apartment. The complex was nice and well-kept, if not fancy. It had a pool and playgrounds for the kids. To get these kinds of amenities in Toronto, you need to be living in a high-rise apartment building.

Brenda and I began looking for work right away. We quickly enrolled Miranda into CSDF's summer school program, which ran for the month of July, and Terence started to attend a free, one-week, half-day camp run by a local church.

Miranda, of course, loved being back in a school environment. In no time, she made a friend. Her name was Shea Rasmus. She was the same age as Miranda and a deaf child of deaf parents. Shea comes from a long line of deaf people on both sides of her family. Her father was Brian Rasmus, a teacher at CSDF. Shea's mother, Sandra Ammons, was a sign language teacher at several nearby colleges. Both were graduates of Gallaudet University and classmates of Gary Malkowski.

The CSDF had summer sign language classes for parents once a week during July, so we attended and started meeting other parents and teachers. Our instructors were two deaf women, Barbie Dike and Sylvia Wood. Both had deaf children who were students at CSDF. They were friendly and welcoming. Sylvia's husband is Max Malzkuhn, whose mother was one of Gary Malkowski's favorite professors at Gallaudet University. I was finding that nearly everyone in the Deaf community had less than "six degrees of separation from" Gary Malkowski. In fact, it was more like "two degrees" most of the time.

We soon discovered that we had a regional accent as far as the ASL we learned in Canada was concerned. When Miranda and the rest of us signed things like PIG or BIRTHDAY or NERVOUS, we were greeted with uncomprehending looks. Soon we were learning northern Californian sign variations. It gave me a good excuse whenever I messed up or used an incorrect sign. I would laugh and sign, OH, THAT'S CANADIAN SIGN!

August, 1996 was a tough month for the Medugno-Paddons. We had moved into our apartment, but summer school was over, so the kids were at loose ends. We also didn't have a lot of money to go traveling about the Bay Area to check out the attractions like first-time visitors would.

We were terribly lonely, and celebrating our children's birthdays with just the four of us at the local Chuck E. Cheese was a low point. It was really depressing. Things got worse when our five-year-old girl threw a fit because all the tickets she earned from playing the arcade games in the restaurant were not sufficient enough to trade in for the toy she wanted. With the screaming kids, noisy arcade, lousy pizza, and the expense, I have come to the conclusion that Chucky E. Cheese restaurants are parental torture chambers. It is not a place to go to if you want to cheer up.

Earning a Living

Finding a job wasn't coming as easy as I had hoped. I don't know why I thought it would be simple. If I was an engineer or a computer scientist, sure it would have been a cinch; but with a B.A. in drama and a decade of working in a nonprofit, I wasn't a hot commodity.

Through a temp agency, I worked for three days in Silicon Valley for a strange Korean company that seemed to be obsessed with security. The position was supposed to last several weeks, but I completed the assignment in a day and a half. Because it would take her awhile to build up her piano-teaching business, Brenda began waiting on tables at a Mexican restaurant called the Luna Loca in the nearby shopping center. In early October, I landed a part-time permanent job at the Fremont Hospital, which was within walking distance from our apartment. The Fremont Hospital is a behavioral health care facility, not a regular hospital. I began working as an assistant in the community relations department, making $11 an hour. My boss was a wonderful woman named Joan Bettencourt (now Newman) who was supportive of me both professionally and personally; we remain friends to this day.

As a lifetime resident of Fremont, Joan was very helpful in educating me about my family's new hometown. As I was admiring Mission Peak on the horizon one day, I asked about hiking to the top of this mountain that overlooks Fremont. Joan told me about Ohlone Community College, which sits in the hills below the peak, and how to navigate the trails that go up to the top.

One fall afternoon, I started up the trail at the base of the mountain, and a couple of hours later, after a fairly strenuous walk, I was at the top of Mission Peak with a gorgeous view of the San Francisco Bay. I wasn't alone at the top, as the hike is a popular local activity. I started talking to an oral deaf man who had just moved to the area as well. I assumed he was in Fremont to work at CSDF, but he was not. He had some kind of high-tech job in Silicon Valley, which we could also see from our vantage point.

Fremont was not a disappointment in regards to the Deaf community and deaf role models. Even at the top of the peak, you could run into someone who was deaf or knew sign language. Almost everywhere we went, we would see ASL being used. This was very comforting and reassuring. It looked like we had made a good decision, moving to northern California.

I wrote an open thank-you letter to the CSDF community, which the school newspaper printed on November 22, 1996. After being in Fremont for only four months, I had not been the least bit disappointed by the school or the city. Seven years later, I still say the same. Fremont has been a good place to raise a family with deaf and hearing children. It is not an inexpensive area or a place without its challenges, but I have no regrets about the leap of faith we took in the summer of 1996 to move to northern California.

Chapter Seven
Kindergarten at CSDF

IN LATE AUGUST, 1996 on the weekend before school began, the California School for the Deaf, Fremont, (CSDF) held an orientation for new students and their parents. Parents who didn't live nearby stayed in the school's residential cottages, the same ones that students stay in during the year. In addition to meeting some of the teachers, administrators, and school staff, parents and students have an opportunity to meet other parents and students.

On a Friday evening, the new families were welcomed to the school with some entertainment, which, if my memory is correct, was called "Deafywood Squares." This was a take-off on the "Hollywood Squares" game show, only all the celebrities were members of the CSDF staff pretending to be someone famous and answering questions that pertained mainly to Deaf culture. It was a fun icebreaker.

On Saturday morning, we attended workshops and a parent panel run by the CSDF outreach department's Hedy Udkovich Stern, where "veteran" parents gave their viewpoints and tips about the school and helping the students succeed. Little did I know then, that in many subsequent years, I would frequently be one of the veteran parents on the panel, speaking to new students' parents about CSDF. I don't believe I was sought after because I was such a great speaker, rather because I was a father, I lived nearby, I was willing, and I could not say no to the adorable Hedy and later the other outreach department family coordinators.

On Saturday afternoon, there was a group swim in the school's Olympic-sized pool. Miranda has always been a good swimmer. She started before she was two years old, taking lessons at the East York Community Center in Canada. So when she was required to pass a swimming test that afternoon in order to be allowed to go into the deep end and jump off the diving board, Miranda did quite easily. When I saw how impressed people were with her ability, I felt proud of her.

On Saturday evening, traditionally, all the new parents and school staff members are invited to the superintendent's home for a reception. Dr. Hank and Bunny Klopping's house is open to the CSDF community several times throughout the year for parties and potlucks. The Kloppings are CODAs (children of deaf adults) and are beloved for their support of the Deaf community, the students, and their families.

Needless to say, after this orientation week, I was more certain that coming to Fremont was the right thing for our family.

The First Day of School

Long before the small school bus arrived to take Miranda to her first day of kindergarten at CSDF, she was up and ready. Most deaf kids love going to a deaf school because it is the one place they can communicate unencumbered with their peers. My daughter is no different. She loves being at school with her friends.

I have priceless videotape footage from 8 a.m. on September 9, 1996 of Miranda impatiently waiting for the school bus. In the video, she stands looking out the window, signing SCHOOL BUS. I don't need the videotape to remember that moment. She wore a short black skirt, a short-sleeved purple flowered blouse, sneakers, her Disney's *The Hunchback of Notre Dame* backpack, and a narrow headband in her short, sun-bleached blond hair. Her skin was tanned from swimming in the complex pool all summer. I was a proud father who thought, "Oh, she is so cute!" Upon viewing the videotape again, I wished I could reach back in time and hug that adorable five-year-old one more time.

I don't have it on videotape, but I do remember when the yellow mini-bus finally pulled into the apartment complex parking lot at around ten after the hour, Miranda was at the door in a flash. She exchanged kisses and signed I LOVE YOU with Mom and Dad, then she was gone. And so it began.

This was the end of the beginning and, of course, the beginning of something entirely new and wonderful: deaf school. Miranda's kindergarten class was a special group (six boys and six girls), half of whom came from hearing families and half from deaf families. Twelve was a good-sized class, and with the many other children in the pre-kindergarten classes, CSDF's early childhood education department had a large pool from which to support variety with peer learning and interaction.

Veteran teachers Nancy Brill and Doralynn Folse teamed up to provide the group of five-year-olds with an exciting and educational year of school. Though both teachers are hearing, they were diligent about signing all the time, and it was only after months of interaction that I realized Ms. Folse was, in fact, a hearing person. Ms. Brill

In October 1997, Miranda and the rest of the first-grade class visit a Fremont firehouse and get to try on some gear.

was very warm and motherly, and Miranda really liked her. The school year 1996–1997 was filled with many amazing as well as mundane learning experiences for the deaf kindergarteners of CSDF. There were field trips and numerous celebrations and special events.

Around Halloween, the kindergarten class took a field trip to nearby Ardenwood Farm, a regional historic site and park in Fremont, where they picked pumpkins straight from a patch. On October 31, my darling daughter wore a bride's outfit to school for trick-or-treating around campus.

Dad steals Halloween candy from The Bride a.k.a. Miranda and a Star Wars *character a.k.a. Terence.*

On Veteran's Day, CSDF is traditionally in session and open to parents and the public. The kindergarten class was part of a performance in the school's Little Theatre. They did handshape stories for the audience. Handshape stories are an American Sign Language (ASL) form of poetry with several variations, but basically it involves telling a story using signs with the same handshape. Miranda was again dressed up for this special public performance. She wore a colorful, flowered dress with white stockings and white closed-toe sandals.

Leave it to a bunch of five-year-olds to steal the Open House variety show. There was just too much cute on that stage for any sane person to absorb without imploding. I had to compose myself a few times as I was tearing up. This experience for Miranda was exactly what we wanted for her and why we moved to Fremont. She was so proud, confident, and happy to be on that stage in front of people, communicating in her natural language.

After the Veteran's Day event, CSDF celebrated Thanksgiving with a feast, where all the children in the early childhood education department dressed up as pilgrims and Native Americans. Wearing a white bonnet and vest made from white construction paper, Miranda made a cute pilgrim. Parents were invited to attend the feast, and I was happy to witness my Canadian-born daughter experiencing a "real American" Thanksgiving for the first time. Canadian Thanksgivings are celebrated in early October without any pilgrim pageantry. Besides that missing element, the holiday is basically observed in the same manner as an American Thanksgiving.

Christmas and New Year in California

Our first Christmas after moving to California was spent in San Diego with my family. It was difficult for Brenda to be away from her family and not have a Canadian chill in the air. It just didn't seem like Christmas to her stuck in the warm sun of Southern California. The kids enjoyed being with their cousins.

As the year 1997 began, the deaf students of the class of 2009 soon celebrated Martin Luther King Day, Chinese New Year, Presidents' Day, and Valentine's Day. Each special day was an event that included many opportunities for learning and exposure to American cultural occasions. Memorable events, preserved on film by Ms. Folse and other amateur school photographers, included trips to the seashore and tide pools, the post office, and Raley's grocery store (a Fremont business that has employed CSDF students in the past).

The Story of Harriet Tubman

With my theatre background, the highlight of Miranda's kindergarten class for me was their production of a play about Harriet Tubman, a former slave who helped start the Underground Railroad, which saved countless of runaway slaves. If I recall correctly, the play was in honor of Black Heritage Month. Unfortunately, there were no African American children in Miranda's class; fortunately the director of the play (Ms. Folse) believed in nontraditional casting, and my little brown-eyed blonde, whose summer tan was long gone, was assigned the role of Harriet Tubman.

Miranda has always been a natural actress and a quick study. While at the Happy Hands Preschool at the Bob Rumball Centre for the Deaf (BRCD), she played Goldilocks in a charming production of "The Three Bears," and the following year, she was Mrs. Claus in a "Rudolph the Red-Nosed Reindeer" show.

Now, this part of Harriet Tubman was a real stretch for her, but she did a great job dancing with her "African" mates who get captured, chained, and sent to America. When she escapes slavery and establishes the safe houses that become stops on the Underground Railroad, she is happy to be free and helping other former slaves. The play ended with a wild celebration as Abe Lincoln says, "I am Abraham Lincoln and you slaves are all free!" Because one of the boys got stage fright, the great president was played by a teacher's aide named Haruko, a deaf middle-aged Asian woman. I couldn't contain my laughter. How far from type-casting can one get than this?!

Pah! Day

Pah! Day, celebrated by CSDF in mid-March, commemorates the Gallaudet University Revolution of 1988, when the college students and Deaf community shut down the university until a deaf individual was hired as the school's president. The students celebrated Pah! Day with a march around the campus, waving "Deaf Pah" signs and wearing self-made paper hats. They chanted in sign: DEAF PRESIDENT NOW! This was the Gallaudet students' demand when they were marching down the streets of Washington, D.C., nine years earlier; but for these young students, it was a statement of fact.

Pah! Day that year was extra special because one of the student leaders, Bridgetta Bourne, had recently joined the CSDF staff. Now married, Bridgetta Bourne-Firl was employed in the school's outreach department. She came to California with her husband Leslie Firl, a CSDF alumnus returning to the institution as a middle school teacher. They relocated from Maryland with their young son at around the same time that we came to Fremont with our family.

Bridgetta Bourne-Firl

We have been fortunate to come in contact with many superior Deaf role models. I have really enjoyed getting to know Bridgetta. In fact, I wrote an article about her in the spring of 1997 for the local *Fremont Argus* newspaper as well as CSDF's *Cal News* newsletter:

In March 1988, Bridgetta Bourne-Firl made headlines in the deaf world's version of the Boston Tea Party. Bourne-Firl and three friends led protests that closed down Gallaudet University in Washington, D.C. for a week until the university hired its first Deaf president. . . .

At the time, Bridgetta Bourne was a junior and the only female of the four student leaders who ran "the fort during the protest," which ultimately led to I. King Jordan being elected the first Deaf president in the university's history. . . .The peaceful protest grabbed national media headlines for a full week as Deaf people dug in their heels and said no to paternalism and being dictated to by hearing people. Bourne was front and center, coordinating the daily rallies and nightly meetings, keeping the rebel leaders and other students united and consistent, "so we all said the same things."

Bourne-Firl recalled, "We had many disagreements [between] the four of us! But I always had the role of trying to pull us all together. I was the least public figure of the four of us."

The students were supported by the Gallaudet Alumni and many hearing people, including congressmen, from all over the U.S. and the world. When the board, made up of mostly hearing trustees, backed down under enormous pressure as a result of savvy media manipulation by the students, a huge victory was realized and a psychological barrier was hurdled by the Deaf community. . . .

"Deaf Pah Day" at the Fremont campus is an annual celebration of DPN [Deaf President Now] recognizing the achievement. "Pah!" is an American Sign Language expression that loosely translated means "victory at last" or "finally!" . . .

Looking back at the events in 1988, Bourne-Firl spoke of the legacy and the importance of the student revolt, "There has been increased awareness in the general community. People are more interested in learning ASL, about Deaf Culture and how to work with Deaf individuals. The DPN movement was the impetus for the passage and implementation of the Americans with Disabilities Act that allows us greater access to public and private services."

Dr. Klopping [CSDF superintendent] said that since coming to the school, Bourne-Firl has been "a force" in getting new workshops and seminars off the ground that educate the people who educate the deaf.

"California School for the Deaf, Fremont was most fortunate to attract to its ranks a very knowledgeable, active Deaf woman.... She is an excellent resource...and a wonderful role model for hearing and Deaf children," stated Dr. Klopping....

"My lifetime mission is to make the lives of Deaf people better. I will always do that no matter where I am or what I do," stated Bourne-Firl.

I felt Miranda was a very fortunate girl to have a role model like Bridgetta on campus. Knowing Gary Malkowski in Canada and now Bridgetta Bourne-Firl in California, you couldn't ask for two better adult role models for your deaf children.

Working Challenges and Changes

I worked in the community relations department at the Fremont Hospital from October 1996 to April 1997. One morning, I gave Bridgetta a tour of the facilities. I made arrangements for her to do an inservice workshop for the hospital staff, which was well attended and appreciated.

The hospital was often the short-term destination for in-crisis deaf students. It was understood that these students and other deaf people would be much better served in a facility that had therapists and nurses who could sign. The Americans with Disabilities Act requires that the hospital provide an interpreter for a deaf patient, but that would often take time to arrange and, of course, cost extra money.

As I lived just walking distance from the hospital, I was once called in to help communicate with a deaf adult, a young woman who was a former CSDF student and was now abusing drugs. The patient refused to cooperate. The staff was waiting for an interpreter to arrive. It broke my heart to see this highly agitated young woman stuck in a small room with a bunch of us hearing people, talking about her and trying to get her to behave appropriately.

I did my best to relay messages back and forth between the staff and the woman. When she began banging on the windows, I begged her to stop because they were going to put her in restraints, which for a deaf person must be the equivalent of a hearing person getting his or her mouth taped shut. Eventually, she calmed down and the interpreter arrived; I left the hospital, shaken and upset. Psychiatric hospitals, jails, and prisons are not good places for people to be, especially deaf people. I do not know what became of this young woman, but I still think about her.

My New Job

As I was only working part-time in the community relations department at the Fremont Hospital, I continued to look for full-time employment. I kept my eye on Silicon Valley and the high-tech products that were coming out, many of which would become very beneficial to the Deaf community.

One product that really got my attention was a new consumer videophone called the ViaTV Videophone, a black box with a camera that sits atop a television on which video images are displayed. Unlike expensive corporate videoconferencing systems that use digital lines, ViaTV units use regular phone lines and cost only several hundred dollars.

Since a long-distance call from family or friends was a nonevent for Miranda, I was very interested in getting a consumer videophone. It pained me greatly to see her left out whenever Terence got on the phone and chatted with his hearing grandparents or friends. I dearly wanted to give Miranda a visual so she could be involved in our telecommunication with extended family members.

I contacted 8x8, Inc., the maker of the ViaTV Videophone, and spoke to the director of communication, Scott St. Clair. I suggested that their product might be a great boon to the Deaf community if the picture quality was good enough for transmitting sign language. St. Clair said they were very interested in tapping vertical (niche) markets as well as the horizontal (broad consumer) ones.

When I asked if I could bring some deaf people down to their offices to try out the equipment, Scott said absolutely. He and his co-workers were excited to see if and how their technology would meet the Deaf community's needs. A few weeks later, I escorted Sylvia Wood and Bridgetta Bourne-Firl to 8x8's Santa Clara headquarters to test the ViaTV Videophones for sign language communication.

The testing of the videophones was a good experience for all. The company learned something about the needs of the Deaf market, and we determined that the phone's picture quality was not sufficient for smooth ASL communication. The videophone product would need some upgrades before 8x8 could tap the Deaf niche market.

While I was there, I slipped my resume to Scott St. Clair, telling him I was looking for a job. A month later, I was hired by 8x8 to be the managing editor of online media, mainly responsible for writing content for their website, user success stories, and customer newsletters. I was sad to leave behind the good people I had met at the Fremont Hospital, but it was time for me to work a full-time job and earn the salary necessary to support a family in the San Francisco Bay Area.

Graduation

Miranda's first year at CSDF went by quickly. Before Brenda and I knew it, we were being invited to a kindergarten graduation ceremony. My darling daughter wore a long-sleeve red velour dress with white tights and shoes. She also wore red gym shorts beneath her dress, a sensible addition for the playground time that was sure to follow the formal event. Miranda wore her black mortarboard almost regally. Brenda and I were so proud of her. She had smoothly made the transition from pre-school to kindergarten, and from Canada to California. I confess I got a little misty as I envisioned her high school graduation. Though still years away, I knew it would come faster than expected.

Chapter Eight
Starting Elementary School

The California School for the Deaf (CSDF) Elementary School serves five grade levels and is located on the north end of campus. The single-floor building is designed with the classrooms on the outside and a central common area called a pod on the inside. There is a pod per every four classrooms. In a nearby separate building, there is an activity center dedicated to the elementary school, which is used for the assembly of the 100 or so students enrolled.

Elementary residential students are housed near the elementary school in dorms, which are called "the cottages" because that's what they look like. CSDF's youngest residential students are around six or seven years old and commute every Sunday evening to the school and return to spend the weekend at home on Friday afternoons.

Students come from all over northern California to attend the deaf school. Residential student life has its advantages and disadvantages. The obvious advantage is that students are in a signing environment the entire time they are on campus, with opportunities to learn and socialize when not in the classroom. The disadvantage is the student misses out on family life and having a parent or two to make sure things are going well. Though the dedicated and underpaid CSDF counselors do their best with their students, they cannot be as good as a parent, in most cases.

I understand every family is different, and not everyone can afford to live in Fremont, the Bay Area, where the cost of living is extraordinarily high; but we felt that our child should spend nights at home. This accommodation comes at a price, but it's important to us, so we willingly pay the cost, as do many other families with students at CSDF.

As a day student, Miranda rode a school bus for a time, but because of logistical problems every year, there was no guarantee that she could be to school in a short amount of time, even if we only lived a mile from the school. On occasion, Miranda's bus rides were taking forty-five minutes to an hour each way. Some students, who lived outside of Fremont, traveled an hour and a half each way.

Another issue with the CSDF buses is that most of the drivers don't know how to sign. The school contracts with an outside company, and though the drivers are generally very good, we didn't like the idea of Miranda and the other deaf kids being alone on a bus for long periods of time without an adult who can speak their language. Fortunately, CSDF does provide chaperones who go on the long rides with deaf students who live hours away and travel on Fridays and Sundays.

Miranda's first-grade teacher was Debbie O'Neill, a hearing woman with a very cheerful, down-to-earth personality and a motherly demeanor. A veteran teacher, Debbie was married to a deaf man and was a mother of several hearing children. She taught the "B" class. We had been warned about the streaming of students, and we were greatly disappointed to find Miranda was not put into the "A" class. Because she was born in late August, Miranda was one of the youngest students in her first-grade class. Some of Miranda's classmates were almost a full year older than she was and were assigned to the "upper" class. This streaming would be a source of irritation for Miranda, Brenda, and me for several years.

We soon learned that streaming is a numbers game: Two teachers are assigned to the first grade to handle twelve to fourteen kids, and there have to be between six and eight kids in each class. Miranda was in the middle as far as academic development in her group. She was considered a borderline child and was placed in the "lower" class, which consisted of a number of rambunctious boys.

We were concerned that Miranda was not going to get as good an education since the B class teacher had to spend so much time and energy disciplining the less-attentive, less-mature, and/or less-intelligent students. Meanwhile, the A class cruised along with the higher functioning kids, going further and further ahead of the B class students, who were being sucked down to the lower level because of the aforementioned issues as well as the teachers' lower expectations.

We did our best to get Miranda moved into the other class, but were not successful until her third-grade year. Miranda helped the cause by working hard and remaining at the top of the B class. We assisted Miranda with her homework and extra assignments and hired a tutor, a young deaf woman named Sha Reins. Miranda liked Sha very much and responded well to the extra attention and work.

Sha was from a deaf family. Her mother, Donetta Reins, was our teacher in the CSDF family ASL classes that were offered on Thursday nights. We really enjoyed getting to know both mother and daughter. They were very supportive of our family, and we missed them when they moved away because of the high cost of living in the Bay Area. They were just a few of the many deaf (and hearing) folks who left the Bay Area for this reason since we moved here.

In Support of Learning ASL

One of the many great things CSDF does for families of students is offer free, evening sign language classes for parents and siblings. I attended these classes faithfully for years. It is kind of embarrassing that after ten years of formal sign classes, I still require instruction. I am sure if she knew, my high school French teacher would not be surprised to hear of my limitations in learning a second language.

At around this time, I was asked by Hedy Stern to write an article for the school's weekly newsletter *Cal News*, which goes home to parents. Hedy wanted me to explain why parents of deaf children should learn ASL. I readily agreed but found each attempt to write such an article nearly impossible, and not because I didn't agree with the idea, but because it seemed just so obvious to me.

By that time, I had been signing with my daughter for five years and had enjoyed a rich, rewarding relationship with her as well as with many other deaf people with whom I had come into contact. You need communication to have a relationship. How could I write an article about something that was so self-evident? It is like trying to explain why American children should learn the English alphabet.

Hedy assured me that there were many parents with kids at CSDF who did not sign and did not see the need to learn. I found this to be shocking and sad. I never actually met these parents. All the CSDF parents I knew had learned ASL or were struggling to learn it better. So with continued encouragement, I finally banged out an article that was printed and received good reviews from the Deaf community.

Below is my favorite paragraph from my article:

> Trying to parent and teach a deaf child without using sign language is like trying to drive a car without a steering wheel. You may get somewhere, but not very quickly, and you will surely go in circles and bump into a lot of barriers along the way. That's a scary ride that too many deaf children and their hearing parents have been advised to take in the past.

In the article, I also suggested that family members who attend ASL classes should go with the proper attitude and respect for their instructors and the language they are learning. This is a major pet peeve of mine. Too many times, I have witnessed individuals exhibiting disrespectful behavior toward ASL, the teachers, and their lesson plans.

I have seen ASL students second-guess a deaf teacher's use of a sign or decline to participate in an activity that would help them learn the language. And then the same students would ask questions like "Why is that the sign?" Or "Why are we doing this?" Or "Why don't they use English structure and word order?"

If I had ever questioned one of my college professors like this, I am sure I would have been verbally ripped to pieces and unceremoniously bounced out of class. And deservedly so. Yet, ASL teachers politely respond or smile and shrug, tolerating this disrespect. Imagine going into French class and asking, "Why do the French use all these different words in different word order?" *Sacre bleu!* You would have "idiot" stamped to your forehead and be asked to depart *tout de suite.*

My advice for anyone trying to learn ASL: "Just accept it—ASL is a different language. Don't try to change it or fight it, just learn it."

In every ASL class in which I have been enrolled, the teacher always has at least two rules: (1) students do not use their voices and (2) students ask the teacher if they have a question about how to sign something. Invariably there are people who just don't get it and insist on talking, chatting, voice interpreting (often incorrectly), and asking their neighbor to "interpret" for them, instead of asking the instructor for clarification.

This behavior is doubly rude because often the deaf instructor is not aware that this chattering is going on. Then the hearing student who is desperately trying to concentrate has to be the "talk police" and shush the distracters or bring it to the teacher's attention.

Advice for parents with deaf children: Don't join an ASL class, unless you want to learn and are willing to respect the pursuit, the language, and the instructor. These classes can be good opportunities to socialize, but remember that what you are doing is vitally important and will provide your deaf child with an avenue of clear, fluid communication with the people that love him or her most.

Marketing Videophones

Working for a high-tech company during the late 1990s dot-com boom in Silicon Valley was very interesting. Though 8x8 wasn't an Internet company, it was certainly influenced by the business culture of the time. There was a fever, probably not unlike the Gold Rush of 150 years before. People were job-hopping for substantially larger paychecks and investing in new companies that had a great concept for using the Internet but no real product or service that surfers would buy. Everyone was looking to make an obscene amount of money in a short amount of time. I did not know much about the business world, but it just all seemed more than a bit crazy to a guy with a drama degree who spent most of his career working for nonprofits.

One of the perks of working for a videophone company was being able to buy the products at a discounted price. Though their picture quality left a lot to be desired (with jerky or pixilated images that were often out of sync with the audio), 8x8's ViaTV Videophones still made a phone call visual for a deaf child. So I bought a number of units for my family and my in-laws. I loved being able to provide Miranda with a view of her grandparents, uncles, aunts, and cousins in San Diego and Toronto.

In February of 1999, the top-rated NBC TV show *ER* aired an episode where one of the characters, Dr. Benton, placed a videophone call to his young deaf son. This exhibition of the current technology was a breakthrough of sorts: Mainstream entertainment was proving and promoting the concept that there is no better way to communicate with young deaf children than visually. I knew this to be true from personal experience.

I knew the standard text-telephone (aka TTY or TDD) was not going to be a good solution for young Miranda. TTYs are basically useless for most deaf children under the age of eight or nine whose first language is ASL for three basic reasons:

1. The child hasn't yet learned to read or write fluently in English.
2. The child doesn't have the dexterity to type quickly and produce an error-free message.
3. The child doesn't have the patience for this stilted form of communicating.

Having virtual visits allowed us to feel more in touch with our families, and there was no need to "warm up" to them when we had actual in-person visits.

Here are some of our family highlights using videophones:

1. Miranda sold Girl Scout cookies to her grandparents.
2. I played video hide-n-seek with Miranda one day when she was sick and stayed home from school. I video-called from my office. (I covered my eyes while Miranda hid; then Brenda moved the camera around as I guessed where our daughter might be hidden.)
3. Frustrated with trying to chat on a traditional TTY, Miranda and a friend who also had a videophone were able to switch to video and plan a get-together.
4. Miranda enjoyed showing off "Student of the Month" certificates and artwork to extended family members.
5. Miranda corrected my father-in-law when he signed I LOVE YOU wrong.
6. On Halloween Miranda was able to display her costume and the pile of candy she got from trick-or-treating.
7. When 8x8 ran a "Call Santa" promotion, Miranda was able to see and show Santa what she wanted for Christmas.

8. On Christmas morning, Miranda was able to show off to cousins the "life-size" Barbie doll she got from Santa.

After witnessing so many valuable interactions, I know videophones have enriched Miranda's life. I believe the following benefits would be true for prelingually deaf children and their families, if they begin using a videophone, webcam, or videoconferencing device:

1. Access to extended family members and events
2. Access to deaf classmates (or Deaf role models, if they are isolated in a hearing-only community)
3. Access to parents at work or home (if the young child is living in a school dorm)
4. Access to more information about the world, in general

Videophones benefit the parents of deaf children by providing:

1. Access to their child if they are at work or the child is away at a residential school
2. Access to an interpreter or Deaf role model for immediate assistance in sign language or other Deaf child issues
3. Satisfaction with themselves for bringing state-of-the-art technology into their children's lives for their direct benefit

Helping Invent a New Product

Due to the limited video quality issues with the ViaTV Videophone, 8x8 wasn't making much headway in selling their product to the Deaf community. (Actually, they weren't selling many to the broad consumer market either.) It occurred to me that it might make sense to offer a videophone with text-chat capability, combining the text-telephone with a videophone. Thus, the idea for the ViaTV VideoTTY was born.

I became one of the three inventors who were listed on the patent that 8x8 submitted and eventually got approved for the VideoTTY (#5,978,014). My co-inventors were Truman Joe and Bryan Martin, the 8x8 engineers who made the product a reality.

The product was pretty slick, if I do say so myself. It looked and functioned the same as the ViaTV models, but also came with a wireless keyboard. Once a user made a videophone connection, he or she could type on the keyboard and see words appear in white type on a blue banner, above the picture being transmitted. The first VideoTTYs to go on the market cost around $350.

We seeded (gave away) a few units with demo families and tried to grow the market and fine-tune the product. Bridgetta Bourne-Firl's family was one of our demo families. Because her family lives in Maryland and she resided in Fremont at the time, I provided both her parents on the East Coast and her family in California with VideoTTY units.

They had some good experiences using the VideoTTY. Bridgetta said that one time, her family members were able to have three conversations at once. She and her mother were signing slowly to each other using the video element, Bridgetta's husband Leslie and her father in Maryland were using the keyboards to carrying on a text-chat, while Bridgetta's hearing son was using the audio from the phone's handset to talk to his hearing aunt on the East Coast.

Unfortunately, the product was a bit cumbersome to set up and use. It wasn't always reliable either because of the quality of the long-distance carrier phone lines or the phone lines within the two households. Sometimes it would take repeated tries to get the videophone units to "handshake," and when it finally did progress to showing an image, the quality of the image would be plain lousy.

Nevertheless, I found the product worked wonderfully most of the time both in my own home and with my dad in San Diego. Since my dad doesn't sign, he really enjoyed chatting using the text-chat capability with Miranda and seeing her at the same time. She enjoyed seeing his face and the faces of other family members, even if the image wasn't clear.

One of the most memorable occasions of using the VideoTTY at home was when my dad (known as "Nonno" to his grandkids) tested Miranda's knowledge of state capitals. He made a flat offer to all his grandkids that if they learned the state capitals of all fifty states, he'd give them $50. When Miranda felt she'd done sufficient studying, we placed a video call to Nonno. He typed the state names, and then Miranda typed the corresponding capital. He gave her a "thumps up," and on it went until she had done all fifty states and won the money.

Joining IMPACT

Marketing videophones to the Deaf community led me to an organization called Independently Merging Parents Association of California (IMPACT), which is an advocacy organization for parents of deaf children in California. Every year, IMPACT and the California Educators of the Deaf (Cal-Ed) organization stage a joint conference for parents, teachers, administrators, and other parties interested in Deaf education.

In March of 1998, the Cal-Ed/IMPACT conference was held at the Doubletree Hotel in San Jose, just down the road from 8x8's Silicon Valley offices. As the Deaf market had been identified as one 8x8 wanted to target, I was asked to join the exhibitors at the conference and demonstrate our video communication products. I hired Donette Reins to sit in front of a videophone at 8x8 and "video visit" with attendees at the conference. It was fun allowing Donette to virtually "meet" old friends via the VideoTTY, but because of the limitations of the video quality, many people didn't initially recognize her, and some thought she was a man. Needless to say, the company didn't have a lot of luck selling VideoTTYs, but for me personally, it was a wonderful experience. I met many fellow parents and sneaked into a few of the workshops, which covered a gamut of topics concerning the raising and educating of deaf children.

I joined IMPACT that weekend and soon found myself sitting on the organization's board. Anyone who knows me, knows I'm not a great "meeting guy," so it was a real challenge for me to attend the quarterly, all-day meetings. But I hung in for three years, helped set up the organization's first website (www.deafkids.org), and served as the IMPACT newsletter editor for a couple of years. Many of the experiences I wrote about for the IMPACT newsletters have been incorporated into this book.

I have attended every Cal-Ed/IMPACT conference from 1998 to 2004, though not as an exhibitor. For a couple years, I helped run the conference. In that capacity, I feel my biggest accomplishments were organizing the Saturday evening entertainments. At the 2000 conference held at the San Francisco Airport Marriott, Hedy Stern and I planned and executed a fun family night of silent films, followed by a Charlie Chaplin impersonation contest for the kids. It was a big hit and the cost to the conference was miniscule.

The following year, the conference was located at Riverside Convention Center. My contribution was to arrange for a screening of the controversial documentary film *Sound & Fury* as the Saturday night entertainment, just days after the movie had been nominated for an Academy Award for Best Documentary Film. It was a real coup. The conference also arranged to fly out from New York one of the co-producers, Jackie Roth, to discuss the film with the audience after the viewing. It was a great event with a profound exchange of thoughts, theories, and feelings by those in attendance. (See my review of *Sound & Fury* in the appendix.)

For the past few years, I have had the pleasure of being a workshop presenter. Brenda and I presented a workshop titled "Games for Deaf and Hearing Children to Play Together Successfully." It was very well received at the 2002 conference in Sacramento. (I have also included the outline of that presentation in the appendix of this book. I hope parents find this information useful.)

My more recent workshops at the Cal-Ed/IMAPCT conferences have been on Gary Malkowski and the issues facing people like me—a hearing father of a deaf daughter. It should come as no surprise that some of that content has found its way into this book.

Chapter Nine
"Did You Want A Deaf Baby?"

WHEN SHE WAS SEVEN YEARS OLD, Miranda surprised me one day while I was minding my own business, reading the newspaper. She interrupted me and asked a question that I was totally unprepared for. She looked at me with her big brown eyes and signed, "Did you want a deaf baby?"

I was still for a moment, almost as if the wind had been knocked out of me. "Oh, my God!" I thought to myself, "What is she asking me? Is she asking what I think she is asking?"

I'm hearing. Her mother is hearing. Her older brother is hearing. We had never known a deaf person in our lives until the day she was born. "What is the subtext of her question?" I thought. My mind raced. "Is she asking if I wanted her? Is she looking for acceptance—unconditional acceptance? Or does she just want to know, in the same way she might have asked, "Did you want a blond-haired daughter or a brown-haired one?"

She stood there in front of me, patiently waiting for an answer. I started to sweat and breathe heavily. My mind was flying through the metaphysical obstacle course. It was a question of great complexity and gravity. I asked myself, "Do I understand the subtext correctly?!"

I nearly panicked as the inner dialogue continued at lightning speed: "Can I separate her from her deafness? . . . Maybe I can, but can she?" I needed time. I stalled, asking her to repeat herself. Maybe I had misunderstood her question. Maybe I wouldn't have to come up with *the* perfect answer today. I needed some time to really mull this over.

Miranda asked again with more emphasis, "Did you *want* a deaf baby?"

"Geez! She wants to know if I wanted a deaf daughter. She really wants to know if I wanted her to be deaf." I am not the sharpest tack in the bulletin board, but I knew I had to give her an answer fast, because not having an answer for her immediately was an answer in itself—a negative one.

The missing teeth twins—Miranda with her best friend Shea Ammons Rasmus in Fremont.

Well, of course, I didn't wish for a deaf baby. But if I told her, "No, I did not want a deaf child," how would that make her feel? I thought, "She's too young to understand, isn't she?" But I didn't want to lie. I didn't want to undermine my trustworthiness. I wanted her to always trust in my word. I wanted to be a good role model for my kids. But if I told her the truth, would I be planting a seed in her beautiful little head that would slowly grow and grow, and then suddenly, years later, spring out with horrible teenage rage: "You don't love me! You didn't want me! You wanted a perfect little *HEARING* baby!"

But what is the real "truth?" I've always believed the truth is in your heart, not your head. And suddenly, a calm settled over me. I didn't need to think anymore. I looked at my beautiful daughter and said what I felt: "Yes." I signed. "Yes, I wanted a deaf baby girl."

Miranda's face lit up and then she was gone as suddenly as she had appeared. I sunk back into my sofa, exhausted from our thirty-second encounter. I was relieved and pleased that I had given *the* perfect answer. Of course I wanted a deaf daughter. I may not have known it at the time, but I know it now. I wanted Miranda. I wanted all the challenges, including learning a new language. I needed to know about people who experience life in a very different way. Having a deaf child has broadened my life and added great depth to my personhood. I've been enriched. Of course, I wanted that. I needed that. I wanted a deaf daughter and I will never regret it.

Miranda's First Summer Camp Experience

In the summer of 1998, Miranda went away to deaf camp for the first time. I was pretty ambivalent about the idea: You drive your deaf kid up a mountain three hours away and drop her off in the middle of the forest to stay with a bunch of strangers for a week. No, I don't think so!

That's one way of looking at summer camp and kind of the way I was feeling about the Lion's Wilderness Camp Sylvester in Pinecrest, California, before my daughter Miranda went there.

It's only natural to be concerned when your kids go away for the first time without you or your significant other. I suppose every parent from the beginning of time has gone through these "going pains." It is important for us and for our kids to have these experiences—especially our deaf kids. They need to know as much as we need to know that they can survive in the world on their own. Granted, one week in the "wilderness" with attentive counselors is not exactly being "on their own," but it's a valid, healthy, and necessary step in that direction.

Still, a little tear was in my eye as we, her mother, her brother and I, said goodbye on that Sunday afternoon in the Sierra Nevada mountain range; we would not see our girl until Saturday. I thought of my father-in-law's joke, "Seven days without Miranda makes one weak." (I believe there are many benefits to being deaf—not having to give courtesy laughs to lame puns is one of them.)

I looked forward to the letters we had primed Miranda to write—seven self-addressed and stamped envelopes were packed into her suitcase. My wife and I had already started sending letters to Miranda before she left, so she'd have something from us during her first days. In with the letter I mailed to Miranda on Monday, I enclosed a stick of gum. I knew when Miranda received it, she would be delighted.

Our first and only letter from Miranda arrived on Friday. It read simply:

To Brenda, Terence and Dad,
I am very miss Mom, Terry, Dad.
Love, Miranda

When we arrived on Saturday morning to pick her up, Miranda hand-delivered six more letters. There was some kind of mix-up about how the postal service worked at the camp. The letters were short, sweet, and read:

- Thank you gave gum. Love, Miranda
- I am finished going horseriding. And all kiks horseriding. Are raining! One boy fell off to horseriding.
- Say Hi my friend and holle my Mom, Dad, Terence [inside a heart drawing] To Mom Dad Terence. Love, Miranda
- [drawing of two girls] M B Miranda Love
- I am miss my Mom, Dad, and Terence I very not like girl two I very like girl three. Love, Miranda
- Wedday night I am play star wars I am Queen Amldula Love Miranda

Her letters obviously didn't tell the whole story of her experience. During the drive home, she reported some of the highlights of her week at camp:

- I caught two big fish, so big the line almost broke.
- On Thursday night, at the dance, I danced with a boy. I don't know his name but he had a dirty face.
- Tuesday lunch, the pizza tasted lousy.

Ah, summer camp: snagging big fish, dancing with dirty-faced boys, and eating lousy pizza. Who could ask for anything more?

Second Grade

In second grade, Miranda remained in the B stream. We were certainly becoming frustrated with the second-class education we thought Miranda was getting by being relegated to the B class.

Miranda's second-grade teacher was Jeanie Marsh, a middle-aged, hard of hearing woman whose Deaf husband, Emory Marsh, also taught at the school. She was nice, but we wondered about her effectiveness, especially having to contend with some rowdy boys. Meanwhile, the A class sailed along, enjoying privileges that Miranda's class did not.

One incident sticks in my mind, though Miranda has forgotten it. The A class had returned from some sort of activity or outing. When Miranda happened by their classroom, they were having ice cream. This really drove home the point to Miranda that she was not with the elite, the privileged crowd. When Miranda told me about this, I certainly saw how it pained her. I tried to mollify her a bit by taking her out for some ice cream, but the hit to her self-esteem was real.

After this visit to the ice cream shop, Miranda wrote me a letter that I cherish. Inside an envelope that had "Dad" and hearts on the front and "I Love You" and hearts on the back, all in pink ink, Miranda wrote:

Thank Dad for pay for ice cream! Dig Why you pay ice cream! Why well student! Why I good! Behavior! Night! Pay dig ice cream? I love Dad! I have someone WELL! TaDa!!! Love Miranda

(I think she wrote "dig" meaning "did," though I'm not really sure. I was sure proud of my second-grader and her ability and desire to express herself in written English, a language she has never heard.)

It didn't matter that she was at the top of her class and "Student of the Month" in her classroom for four months out of the nine-month school year, Miranda was getting the message daily that she wasn't as good as the children in the A class. Brenda and I would continue to gently lobby for our daughter to be elevated to the "upper" class, but without immediate success.

When Brenda became a teacher's aide at the deaf school, she became an insider and got an insider's view. She saw how students were labeled. Unfortunately, biases and prejudices are common with administrators and teachers. The notion that deaf kids who have deaf parents are going be brighter and better students leads to a certain amount of bias against students whose parents are hearing.

The idea behind this is that deaf of deaf are getting language, generally American Sign Language (ASL), from birth, while deaf of hearing are language-deprived for months, and sometimes years, until diagnosis, acceptance, and intervention. As with any generalization, there is something to the logic; but when it's applied without much discretion, some kids suffer. This is where parents have to be advocates for their child. Unfortunately, this is the way of the world, not just in deaf education. In general, parents who are involved and pushing for the best for their children are going to have more successful students.

Speech Assessment

In the fall of 1998, Miranda's speech was assessed by the school's audiologist. Though we had long ago accepted that she may never speak well, Brenda and I still had hope that she'd be able to acquire some speech. The assessment report read:

> Based on the test results, Miranda showed very limited ability to produce speech sounds or to use auditory input in simple discrimination tasks. The recommendation of the Communications Department is that Miranda not participate in the speech instruction program. Her time would be better spent in the classroom, developing her reading and writing skills and her general knowledge of the world.

We were not and could not be upset with this assessment. In fact, it might have been a relief, because it confirmed that we made the right choice to focus on visual language. Had we gone the auditory-verbal route, Miranda would have spent too much precious time in a futile effort to acquire speech.

On Miranda's final second-grade report card, teacher Jeanne Marsh wrote:

> Miranda is attentive and responsive to class instruction and has shown a positive and constructive attitude in all areas. She always tries to do her best work. She should be encouraged to read at a higher level. She perseveres and completes the work even if the work is challenging. She is a friendly person and is always willing to help other students.

Laid Off from 8x8

In April of 1999, I was laid off from my marketing job at 8x8. It was disappointing and surprising to me. The pace in Silicon Valley is fast, and with companies like 8x8, the culture is "what have you done for me lately" and "we don't have time to grow a business."

There were a couple of other issues that had prevented us from getting the VideoTTY out into the Deaf community. One was the price. At over $300 a unit, it just wasn't feasible for people to buy one, let alone two, since two units are required to carry on a conversation. Another problem had been the aforementioned poor video quality, which was bad enough at times that it was difficult to discern what the person on the other end might be signing.

We had met with and demonstrated the product for California's Deaf and Disabled Telecommunication Program (DDTP) several times, trying to get their committees to add the product to their program so it could be freely distributed to deaf Californians, but we couldn't get around yet another big problem (after video quality and price) with the VideoTTY: compatibility with non-video TTYs (also known as TDDs).

People at 8x8 thought it was possible to make the product TTY-compatible, but the company hadn't been willing to invest the man hours and money to do it until there was a firm commitment in the form of a large number of orders to make it feasible. It was a catch-22 that couldn't be solved.

Still, I plugged away at marketing the product, hoping for one big program or sale to add momentum and help establish the VideoTTY. I had focused on hearing families with deaf children like my own, because of my own rich experience with the product. But the market hadn't been big enough for the product, and 8x8's commitment had waned. So I guess I should not have been surprised when the axe fell.

Still, it threw me for a loop. I'd never been laid off before. I got a nice severance and was only out of work for about five weeks. I negotiated a better salary than I had before and went to work for InnoMedia, another Silicon Valley startup, marketing their set-top consumer videophones. Whereas 8x8 was entirely dedicated to manufacturing and marketing videophones, InnoMedia had several product lines, mainly concentrated in the Voice-over-Internet Protocol (VOIP) industry. At InnoMedia,

I was the videophone guy, responsible for all marketing aspects of the InfoView consumer videophone. I continued to be an evangelist for videophones and looked forward to the day when Miranda would be chatting with all her friends over a phone network using ASL.

Chapter Ten
Joining the "A" Class

IN THE FALL OF 1999, our lobbying efforts finally paid off and Miranda was elevated to the A class of the third grade. Her teacher was Julie Baer, a young deaf woman who Miranda really liked. We were thrilled that Miranda responded to the challenges, demands, and higher expectations of the A class and more than held her own.

One of the highlights of the 1999–2000 school year was Miranda appearing on the California School for the Deaf's (CSDF's) Little Theatre stage again. During the holidays, the elementary school staged a version of *The Nutcracker.* The play had some dance routines, most of which were not ballet, if I remember correctly. Each grade was responsible for a certain portion of the play. Miranda was very disappointed to be cast as a dancing Christmas tree. She really wanted to play a little girl or a butterfly.

I will never forget the magic of our adorable dancing Christmas tree, which was more like a walking tree with toes pointing up after each step forward. Miranda was precious in her tree outfit, though she still harbors resentment about that experience. On occasion now, to tease her, I will suddenly break into the dancing Christmas tree dance and Miranda will fly into a violent rage and chase me around the house.

Miranda Becomes Randi

When Miranda was born, Brenda and I had not yet decided on a name for our baby girl. I remember sitting in our bedroom the day after her birth, throwing names out. I liked the name Miranda because there was a character in Shakespeare's *The Tempest* called Miranda.

One of the reasons Brenda liked Miranda was because the shortened form could be Randi. When Miranda learned this, at around the end of third grade, she decided she wanted to be known as Randi. Well, actually, she started out as Randy. She made a natural assumption that Randy is a feminine name like Mandy or Brandy. We had to explain to her that the name Randy is generally a boy's name. She, of course, was very perplexed by this. English is so inconsistent, it is a wonder any nonnative speaker can master it.

Eventually, she did adopt Randi as her nickname. Her name sign changed from a shaking "M" to a shaking "R." (Name signs are signs used in ASL in lieu of fingerspelling out a person's full name.)

Her friends now call her Randi, but most of the time, her mother, brother, and I still call her Miranda. Fortunately, when we use her formal name out loud to refer to her, it doesn't bother her because she doesn't hear us. Initially, she would get angry if we wrote or fingerspelled "Miranda" instead of "Randi," but years later, now that her nickname has become firmly established, she will respond and accept either version.

Nancy-Tracy and Other Small Rodents

At around this time, my kids started clamoring for a pet, and because we lived in an apartment, we couldn't get a dog or a cat. I am not big on pets. We had dogs in my family, and all I remember about them was picking up crap in the backyard or chasing the dogs all over the neighborhood when they got loose. Brenda had a good experience with her family's beloved black Scottish Terrier named Duffy.

When a young woman at my office came in with a dwarf hamster, saying she had several more at home that she needed to find new homes for, I broke down and volunteered to take one home to the kids. My kids absolutely loved the small gray and white dwarf hamster. Terence named the hamster Nancy, and Miranda named it Tracy. This is one of the benefits you can enjoy when you have a deaf child and a hearing child—your pets can have two names and there is no fighting about what to call it.

When we spoke to Terence, the hamster's name was Nancy. When we signed to Miranda, we fingerspelled "Tracy." It was a nice arrangement, but it didn't last long. Several weeks later, after a visit to Miranda's school on a "show-and-tell" Friday, Nancy-Tracy died on Saturday. We learned that hamsters are susceptible to drafts. The kids were heartbroken. Miranda in particular was devastated. She wrote Tracy a note, which read:

> Jan. 31, 2000
> Dear Tracy,
> My favorite you than all world! I miss you!
> I love you. You are died. I cries many.
> Love,
> Miranda

We had a small service and buried Nancy-Tracy. When Miranda went back to school and told her classmates the bad news, they were all upset, and this led to each child recalling a passed pet and tears being shed anew.

About a month later, we bought another hamster. Miranda named him "Charlies." Terence didn't get involved so much with this hamster, perhaps not wanting to get attached to another hamster that might die on them. In the first written communication I had witnessed ever between my kids, Miranda wrote a note to Terence:

> To: Terence,
> You like hamster? Yes No
> From, Miranda

Terence circled "Yes" and handed it back to his sister.

Miranda took good care of Charlies. Months later, during the summer, we took him to San Diego with us because we didn't want to leave him alone for a week. He seemed to enjoy life in my Dad's garage, but then died during the drive home through the San Joaquin Valley, succumbing to temperatures in the 100-degree range while riding in our non-air-conditioned car. I think when Miranda looks back, she'll point to this as the time when she learned the most about death.

Charlotte's Web

One of the highlights of my daughter's third-grade year was her acting as Charlotte the Spider in a staged version of the classic child's story *Charlotte's Web*. In an excellent costume designed and made by Brenda, Randi played Charlotte the Spider brilliantly. I couldn't take my eyes off of her.

Miranda had a very heartfelt reaction to the story, and this is perhaps why the teachers cast her into the lead role. The decision to stage *Charlotte's Web* came after the book was read to the third-grade B class by teacher Kathy Greene. The evening after learning the end of the story, Randi sat down and wrote a letter to Ms. Greene:

Dear Kathy,   April 10, 2000
        at night
    I sad in my heart because you story about Charlotte is died. I not want herd that! I love Charlotte because Charlotte is sweet and nice. When Charlotte born 514 sac then Charlotte feeling look like old. Then she died at fair. No one with her when she died. Means I feel not good. I cry, cry, cry and cry. I can't and hard for me. I want stop but miss. Sad story because spier alive short. I hope tomwwrow nice story have good times! My heart is cry too!
From,
Miranda Medugno

Again, I was proud of how my daughter was able to express herself in her second language with only a few errors.

When Cousin Daniel Died

The summer of 2000 turned out to be a sad one for us. While both kids were away at the Lion's Wilderness Camp Sylvester for Deaf Children in Pinecrest, California, my twelve-year-old nephew Daniel drowned in a freakish backyard pool party accident. My sister and I had planned that coming weekend to have our families meet half way between our home in Fremont, California, and their home in Portland, Oregon. We were going to visit Crater Lake and the Oregon Caves. Due to the terrible turn of events, we ended up driving all the way to Portland.

Brenda and I left early Saturday morning to pick up the kids at camp. Many emotional hurdles lay in front of us; the first one was telling the kids the bad news. It was so very sweet to see the children after they'd been gone for a week and, of course, in light of what had happened to my nephew. It should not have surprised me that the children's reaction to the horrible news was one of subdued emotion. They were confused, concerned, and mostly disappointed. Neither my eleven-year-old nor my nine-year-old could fully process that a twelve-year-old, who knows how to swim, could drown.

As we drove, I had plenty of time to think about the drowning. I wondered if the results might have been different if the parents at the pool party had been deaf. My nephew passed out in a four-foot-deep above-ground pool, while his friends played happily, not noticing. Hearing parents might rely on the sounds of kids playing in the water to ensure that they were not in danger, while they left the area for a moment or two. Deaf parents would have had to actually keep an eye on the pool, be less tempted to leave the area unattended by an adult, and likely have noticed the boy floating face down in the pool sooner. Maybe soon enough for him to have been revived without brain damage occurring. Think about this example the next time someone suggests that deafness is "less than." Sometimes less is more.

Our hearts were heavy as we drove past our planned meeting spot, Medford, Oregon. I was worried about how the kids would cope once we arrived in Portland. Terence would surely be affected because Daniel was his buddy. Miranda was a concern too because she would be surrounded by a large group of extended and emotional all-hearing family members, none of whom could communicate fluently with her in sign language. Her extreme isolation in the situation was a possibility we had to work hard to avoid. I don't know how successful we were. Though we did our best to make conversations and events accessible, Miranda spent most of the time at my sister's home just playing with Barbie dolls in a back bedroom.

As it turned out, Miranda was not the only mourner present with a hearing impairment. Daniel's grandfather on his father's side was equipped with a cochlear implant. Jack Schroeder knew a little sign language, which Miranda would confirm later as "very little." I noticed that Jack was being left out of conversations when more than one-to-one communication was occurring. At times, I saw him fake understanding. My wife and I immediately began to assist the group in making Jack more included, by making sure he could see our faces when we were speaking, by speaking clearly, and by giving visual clues. He gave us some insight into his experience of being discriminated against in the workplace because of his hearing loss. He spoke in depth about the embarrassment of saying the wrong things at the wrong times, even after receiving the implant.

The best memory I have of this awful experience was the thoughtfulness and dignity of my sister Marisa, who, in the depths of grief for her beautiful departed son, thought of Miranda when planning the funeral service. She asked her church to provide an ASL interpreter. I hope all deaf kids have extended family members who are as caring about making family events accessible for them. Miranda's eulogy for her cousin Daniel was touching: "He was very sweet. He didn't get mad at me when I broke his Legos."

Chapter Eleven
Famous Folks
and the Fourth-Grade Boycott

CALIFORNIA SCHOOL FOR THE DEAF (CSDF) elementary school instructor Ed Copra, Miranda's fourth-grade teacher, was a hearing man who had been a teacher at the school for more than twenty years. Though we found him a little on the eccentric side, both Brenda and I liked Ed. Other parents with children in his classes over the years and some of his colleagues didn't always share our view.

Randi enjoyed having Mr. Copra as a teacher. They had a good relationship, and she had a pretty good year being in the A class again. One memorable activity: She kept a lively dialogue journal going between herself and Ed that I enjoyed perusing. Randi wrote about Britney Spears, her new hero, and teased Ed about his confession of having a fondness for Jennifer Lopez. I think Ed eventually regretted revealing this fact and was a bit embarrassed when he opened the journal one day to find Miranda had pasted in a glossy, full-color magazine cutout of J-Lo in her famous low-cut dress.

Randi wrote in the dialogue book next to the photo:

3/29/01

Dear Copra,

I hope JLo like you when you met her. Me are right??? I think so you hope it. JLo will say, "Why not you married me because Jlo's boyfriend is break with boy friend. Then both can go to the Hawaii. I hope do it. But maybe not really happen....Do you still fall in love Brietny Spears or what?

(Below are balloon captions that Randi connected to the Jennifer Lopez picture.)

Let join my dance night, Copra! I promise will we not break! I still love you! I not want break! I not want fall in love other woman!

4-2-01
Dear Randi,
Your note made me laugh so hard! I will ask J-Lo if she wants to go to Hawaii with me. What if she says "YES" I love you!

4-2-01
Dear Copra,
Jlo will say yes! I think so! ☺ Look Jlo's body is sexy!

(More balloon captions from another Jennifer Lopez photo wearing the famous revealing dress exposing cleavage and navel.)

Thank you! Welcome me! Because my dress is Hawaii! Oh yes I want go to Hawaii. I love Edward. I never go to the Hawaii.

4-3-01
Dear Randi,
Thank you for the Hawaii dress picture of J-Lo. It probably is true but I would NOT use the "s" word.

I am excited about Hawaii! I will wear my Hawaiian shirts and shorts! It will be hot I hope. J-Lo will love it too!

As a writer, I felt very happy to see my daughter communicating via the written word and having fun doing it. Unfortunately, the media and celebrity influences over even deaf kids was hard to limit. A girl could do worse than Jennifer Lopez as an idol, and Randi had found one in Britney Spears.

Britney Spears

It sounds like a headline for a *National Enquirer* story or a backhanded insult: "Britney Spears: Deaf Girl's Favorite Singer." At the turn of the century, it seemed there was no getting away from the blond Louisiana vixen, and my nine-year-old daughter was not immune to the captivating spell that Britney Spears had on little girls at the time.

For awhile, we had one bedroom in our home that was an astonishing shrine to all things Britney. The walls were covered with Britney posters, Britney collages, and even, for goodness sake, Britney Spears valentines. Let's not even get into all the products and toys endorsed by the showy, honey-haired pop tart. We were drowning in Randi's adoration for this saucy singer.

Oh, I know some of the uninitiated think I'm exaggerating about the breadth and depth of the reach of Britney at that time. Let me assure the doubters, however, Britney was a force in my daughter's life, possibly even an evil one. Though she'd never heard a word sung by Britney, Randi wanted to buy a Spears CD.

Imagine the scene, if you can, of a patient but frazzled father in the music aisle at a nearby Target department store, arguing with his daughter about the purchase of a $15 *Oops, . . . I Did It Again* compact disc:

DAUGHTER (*in sign language*): I want this.
DAD (*in voice and sign language*): Why?!!!
DAUGHTER (*rolling eyes with a "Dad's a dork" expression*): It's Britney
    Spears.
DAD (*with calm sensitivity*): But it's music. You can't hear it.
DAUGHTER (*angrily*): I can if I turn it up loud.
DAD (*angrily*): Ahhh! But then I will have to hear it. Everyone in the
    neighborhood will have to hear it!
DAUGHTER shrugs.
DAD buckles and reaches for the wallet.

So what did my deaf preteen see in Britney? It took a long time, many threats of extra homework, and promises of treats before I could wheedle out an answer. The answer came in the form of an e-mail, as if it was something she couldn't express face-to-face because I was so dense and needed to see it in written form. My daughter wrote, "Britney is a very good singer, dancer and she is pretty!"

Of course, I understand how my daughter can appreciate Miss Spears's dancing and her pulchritude. I certainly share in this appreciation, though I do wish Britney would dress a bit more conservatively. I often feel, after being confronted with the latest Britney photo, the need for a cold shower and an hour's worth of meditation to get the impure thoughts out of my head.

There's nothing wrong with good, old-fashioned sex appeal, but when your child worships someone who claims in words and deeds to be a wholesome virgin, yet dresses like—well, you know—a confusing and wrong message is being sent to girls, boys, and middle-age dads.

Like a *60 Minutes* investigative reporter, I tried to corner my daughter with a question: "So how does a deaf girl know Britney is a good singer?" Randi flat-out refused to elaborate. Maybe no elaboration was necessary. "Well, geez, isn't it obvious?! She wouldn't be famous and ubiquitous unless she was good, would she? Well, would she?!" Ultimately, I guess it was not important to Randi or any of Britney's fans if she was a good singer or not. She was a "pretty" package.

Things got really bad when my Britney-brainwashed youngster began informing people that her last name was Spears! Kids today and their heroes! . . . Why, when I was ten years old, I was a big fan of Boston Red Sox captain Carl Yastrzemski. I had Yaz's Topps baseball card and a plastic Red Sox batting helmet. That was it. . . . And I walked twelve miles to school through three feet of snow in San Diego, but I never considered changing my last name to Yastrzemski.

I was relieved when Randi moved on to an Olsen twins obsession. Though nearly as ubiquitous as Britney Spears, at least Ashley and Mary-Kate are more sweethearts than sassy tarts.

Deaf or Blind People Cannot Be Judges

There are a number of famous deaf female role models who receive a fair amount of national media coverage that a parent can refer to: Linda Bove, Phyllis Frelich, Marlee Matlin, Terrylene (a fellow IMPACT board member), Deanne Bray, and, most recently, Shoshannah Stern (a CSDF graduate and Hedy and Ron Stern's daughter) are all Deaf actresses who have made it to the big time and represent the community well. One famous deaf woman who is cited often for her achievement of winning the "Miss America" pageant is Heather Whitestone.

In 1994, when Heather Whitestone was crowned Miss America, I used a homesign to describe the significance of Heather's achievement to my three-year-old Miranda. I dubbed Ms. Whitestone "the deaf queen."

I did not watch the pageant that year, and was oblivious to the event until I read about it in the newspaper the next day. I can still remember being elated and walking on "cloud nine" as I passed *Toronto Sun* newspaper stands and saw Heather's beaming smile on the front page. I couldn't wait to get home and tell Miranda the news.

I know beauty pageants are a ridiculous American convention that are of questionable value, but it is certainly an achievement for a "disabled" woman to compete in, much less win, such a competition. I suppose it meant more to me than it did to Miranda. The idea that my daughter could be a beauty queen, if she wanted to, was an inspiration.

Six years later, I was sentimental about that time and my silly daydream of having a beauty queen daughter, but it struck a nerve when I read a newspaper article that described how the Miss America organization was going to open a judging position to someone from the general public. However, they made it clear that the judge would have to be able to see and hear all the contestants to make it fair. The reporter put it rather indelicately, but accurately, that "the blind and the deaf need not apply."

The irony struck me hard. Here the Miss America organization was saying that Heather Whitestone, former Miss America, couldn't be a judge. I immediately fired off an e-mail to the officials running the beauty contest, criticizing their backward mindset and lack of character. Below is their unrepentant response:

Dear Richard,

Thank you for contacting the Miss America Organization, and expressing your comments and concerns regarding the Instant Celebrity Judge Contest. When Bob Renneisen was asked about the rules of the contest, he replied that the Instant Celebrity winning Judge must meet the requirements of any Miss America Judge. This would include being able to both see and hear a contestant, and would ensure a fair performance evaluation during competition. He did not state that the "blind and deaf need not apply." This comment was paraphrased and taken out of context by one media source.

As always, the Miss America Organization strongly supports individuals who are physically challenged. Mr. Renneisen has issued the following statement:

In fairness to the contestants competing for the title of Miss America 2001, the Instant Celebrity Judge must meet all of the qualifications of Miss America Judges. Therefore, it is reasonable that the person chosen be able to see and hear the performances of the contestants competing on stage.

Again, thank you for taking the time to contact us on this issue, and on behalf of the Miss America Organization, I apologize for the misunderstanding.

Sincerely,

Kristin Weissman

Public Relations Manager

I guess Heather Whitestone will never be a Miss America Judge until the outdated organization gets a new outlook. Or may be it would be better if it just went away all together, like goldfish-eating contests.

Literacy

Though she was lagging behind her hearing peers, Miranda's literacy development pleased me. She had always liked books and now was into reading the graphic novels in the Elfquest series of books. These novels are full of colorful, detailed pictures, and the stories about elves in medieval times had high drama in them. Later, she and Terence would both graduate to Archie comic books.

As a writer, I place a special value on the written word and knowing that writing is going to be the major avenue of communication between my deaf daughter and the hearing world, I certainly champion her accomplishments.

Witness these precious writings from my pre-teen about her life and loves:

I love Britney Spears!!!!! My favorite pet is hamster!!!!! It is cute!!!!! I have two hamster. One is a boy name Charlies and one girl name Sabrina!!!! They can't be together in cage because they will fight!!!! Because Charlies stay here for one year and Sabrina recently bought. So have to have two different cages. I wish I am become teen!!!!!! I will teen whatever!!!!!!!! I love Britney Spears because she is a cool person!!!!! And she is singer!!!!!

I love to best friends!!!!! My best friend is Shea!!!! Friends is important!!!! I hate in world is K. because she is mean and rude!!!! I went to girl sonut camping. I sleep at tent!!! I not like C. because she is mean and dumb!!!!! The end by Randi Medugno Smile!!!!

Below is one of my favorites of Miranda's stories. For a class assignment, she wrote the following semi-autobiographical account of the ants in our house:

Once upon a time when I was five years old, I woke up and I was hungry. So I went downstairs. I couldn't believe my eyes when there were ants in the kitchen! I cried and my dad, my mom and Terence woke up. "Did Miranda get hurt?" they wondered. My dad walked quickly down the stairs. I ran to my dad. Then my dad saw approximately 2,000,000 ants! My mom saw approximately 30,000,000,000 ants. Then my mom said "I can't cook or eat breakfast. This means Richard must kill all the ants!!!" The end.

I like the difference in my wife's and my estimates on the number of ants: Two million versus thirty billion. Sometimes in real life, my wife and I do have widely divergent perspectives on things. Maybe it's a girl versus guy thing?

In December of 2000, when Randi was nine-years-old, she still believed in Santa Claus. She wrote Santa the following letter. In it, she refers to me playing Santa Claus for "hospital kids." This is one of my proudest accomplishments during my short career of marketing videophones. I set up a program where the company I worked for donated videophones to six children's hospitals around the United States. During the holidays, sick kids were able to dial into the "North Pole" and have a video visit with Santa Claus. I finally put that drama degree I earned from U.C., Irvine, to use and had a blast doing it.

Dear Sanata,

I want give are Dog Robot. Do you finish saw before? I'm girl yellow hair brown eye. I have 2 brother and 1 sister. [She's counting her pet hamsters as siblings!] All my family are hearing especially. I'm are deaf! Do you like north ploe? It's cold! Do you saw many winter anaiml alive in North Ploe? My dad finished play like Sanata for hospital kids. It is very nice right? Why my Dad play like Sanata because he skillful play!!! I'm 9 years old. That know your deer have deer's favorite food is Oat. I can't wait for Christmas!   Love, Randi Medugno

Problems in Copra's Class

Unfortunately, Mr. Copra and a male student began to have personality conflicts, which, over the course of several months, grew into mini-wars of will that disrupted the education of Miranda and her classmates. One of the problems with having a small number of students within classes is that the simple solution of transferring a disruptive student to a different class isn't always acceptable. Copra's class was the A class, and going down to the B class was something neither the school nor the parents wanted.

School principal Eugene LaCosse, Ed Copra, and the student's parents apparently met several times to resolve the issues without success. During this time, Miranda's classroom became more and more disrupted. Miranda and the other students began to come home complaining of problems between Copra and the boy.

In November, a meeting was held at the school for all the parents with students in Copra's classroom, along with Copra and LaCosse. The agenda was not specifically to discuss the problems between the boy and the teacher, but to talk about how parents could assist Copra's class. Not yet privy to the extent of the problems, I was surprised to see how angry two deaf parents were with Copra. They were mad at the way he "flicked a finger" on kids' heads to get their attention or as a reprimand for misbehavior. Though a bit "old school" for my tastes, I didn't find the offense, which Copra freely admitted to, as that big of a deal.

The meeting concluded with a plan for parents to volunteer more time in Copra's class to assist with students and help put a damper on disruptions. I think most of us left the meeting with the impression that things would get better. They didn't. In fact, things got worse.

As the disruptions escalated and more parents in the classroom witnessed problems, e-mails were sent and phone calls were made between the parents and the elementary school staff. My position, which I believe most of the other parents shared, was that the disruptive student needed to be moved out the class immediately. I know now I was naive to think that it could happen just like that. Even more than mainstream schools, state special schools have their bureaucratic red tape to deal with, including forms and IEPs (individual education plans) that all disabled students must have as mandated by federal law. I may have also been incorrect in assuming that the deaf parents with the disruptive son were opposed to moving their child and rather wanted the teacher moved.

I learned again that one of the problems with e-mail is that it can have a life of its own and travel to other unintended readers. If you know so-and-so is going to read it, you might phrase things differently or write with more sensitivity and care. Needless to say, my e-mail, which was fairly critical of the deaf parents, ended up being read by them, and they were not happy with me.

At the time, I didn't really care. I was getting pretty annoyed that my daughter's education was being sidetracked by the constant battle between this student and Mr. Copra. And it certainly seemed like CSDF wasn't acting fast enough to solve the problem.

During the Christmas vacation, some of the parents, including Brenda and I, got together and decided that the best thing we could do was to boycott the fourth-grade A class until the issues were resolved. Since our home was within spitting distance of CSDF, it became the new home school for five or six students from Copra's class when the school session resumed in early January 2001.

Tragically, the day before our boycott was to begin, there was a horrible mini-bus accident that killed a CSDF student and a counselor and put another student in the hospital with serious injuries. The accident occurred when the bus was bringing residential students back to campus from their central California coast homes on highway 101. It was heartbreaking and the entire CSDF campus was in shock the following day.

Though the problems in Mr. Copra's class were not a priority that day, we still went ahead with the boycott. Brenda and a few other mothers homeschooled the students at our house. I sent a letter to the school administration stating the reasons for our actions and enumerating what we wanted to see changed, mainly that the disruptive student be removed immediately.

For two days, Mr. Copra had three students instead of eight in his classroom. Some of the parents, particularly the Deaf ones, were concerned with our actions being perceived as insensitive while the community was in mourning. Again, at the time, I wasn't concerned about perceptions. I wanted the problem solved.

The school finally agreed to move the student. All the parents, except for the mother and father of the disruptive student, met with Eugene LaCosse and his boss, the dean of instruction, Pat Moore. It was an emotional, but helpful, meeting where Ms. Moore learned the full extent of the problem and our dissatisfaction. Both LaCosse and Moore were relatively new in their positions at the time, and I think this experience seasoned them some.

Other Memorable Times in the Fourth Grade

The rest of the school year for the fourth-grade A class went relatively smoothly. One fond memory was "Dingo Night" at CSDF, run by the Associated Parents, Teachers and Counselors (APTC) as a fundraiser. Dingo is a Deaf version of the game Bingo, which uses a deck of regular playing cards instead of Bingo cards and numbered balls. APTC has used Dingo Nights as a fundraiser twice a year since the late 1990s. The typical turnout is seventy people, and the cost to play is $10 for adults and $5 for students.

The Medugno family has attended Dingo Night since its inception, each time winning at least one of the six games or door prizes. We have actually been dubbed "the family that always wins" by other regular Dingo-goers. It's embarrassing and freaky, actually.

Miranda wrote about one of our experiences on February 20, 2001:

My family and I went to "Dingo." I win....I get a Target gift card. Then my brother win....he get gift card bookstore. Then my Dad win!...He get $10 for video....But my Mom not won!

Brenda has since been dubbed "the big loser" of the family, even though she has won at other Dingo Nights. At the most recent Dingo, Randi won a giant, three-foot-high stuffed mouse. We've been trying to get rid of it ever since. Even the local hospital wouldn't accept it for their pediatric ward.

Another fond memory I have occurred in the spring, when I helped chaperone Mr. Copra's class to an Oakland A's baseball game, where the students met up with their pen pals from a local mainstream elementary school. I can never forget Ghirardelli Chocolate Day at the Oakland-Alameda Stadium. Every baseball fan entering the park received a handful of chocolate squares. Well, it was a sunny, warm, eighty-degree California afternoon, and soon melted chocolate was everywhere. Our students were a sticky mess when we finally filed out of the stadium, but they had a good time.

Chapter Twelve
Fifth Grade and Elementary School Graduation

RANDI'S FIFTH-GRADE INSTRUCTOR was first-year teacher Vanessa Sandez, who was perky, cute, and just graduated from college. As Vanessa's first class of students, I'm sure Randi and her classmates (four boys and four girls) will always hold a special place in her heart. I think because of Vanessa youth, enthusiasm, and sweet disposition, the students adored her and will always have fond memories of their last year in elementary school.

Fortunately, this school year was one without major problems between teacher and students. There were, however, issues between students. Miranda began having serious conflicts with another girl in the class. Much of it amounted to the typical problems that girls that age have, squabbling with each other about who is in and who is out of the clique.

Actually, the problems between the girls seem to have started a year before. Witness this note Randi wrote to herself on September 22, 2000:

> My best friends are J. and N. But B. and S. not my friends....Because I knew that they are hate me! So I fair to they not friends with them that why! J. and N. are sweet in the world!!! B. and S. are dumb in world!!! The End!!!

A year later, alliances had switched 180 degrees. Now J. and N. were not Randi's friends, S. was, and B. had moved away. These conflicts spilled over frequently into class and onto the Internet after school hours. Because of their limitation in English and the nature of e-mail, there were many misunderstandings in electronic conversations among the girls. Randi and this one girl continued to have problems, which escalated into a threat to kill my daughter at an evening field trip to the haunted house in Fremont's Hub Shopping Center. The death threat by this ten-year-old girl was probably not serious, but in the shadow of Columbine and other recent school tragedies, it was something not to be ignored either. So I attended the field trip with my daughter and kept an eye on things.

Later, I made the mistake again of e-mailing my concerns to the school and copying the message to the parents of the girl who made the threat. Vanessa was appropriately concerned, and with her assistance, the school started having all the fifth-grade girls meet with the counseling department to resolve issues and help the girls get along better.

However, the father of the girl who made the threat was not happy with me. As he is hard of hearing, he called me up on the TTY and cussed me out. He objected to my getting the school involved and said I should have called him first before sending an e-mail. Maybe he had a point, except that the problem wasn't just an isolated incident, and I didn't have a very high opinion of his and his wife's lax parenting style. (We had too much contact with this child in the past and saw her as basically as a "wild child" who needed discipline and boundaries that the parents seemed incapable of providing.)

So once again, I wasn't very popular with someone in the Deaf community. This was not the first time and probably will not be the last.

Monitoring My Deaf Child on the TTY and IM

As a result of these and other electronic communication problems, I decided I should know a lot more about what my daughter was doing on the phone line and the Internet. As the hearing parents of a deaf child, my wife Brenda and I are constantly confronted with child-rearing problems that we need to respond to, and we're never quite sure if we're responding in an appropriate manner.

Being the parents of our hearing child Terence, there are times when we're not sure if our actions will lead to the desired results. However, if we search, we can easily get a lot of different opinions from family, friends, the community, or media. The same is not true for issues with our deaf daughter.

For example, TTY conversations pose a problem. When Terence is on the phone, I can eavesdrop on his conversation and monitor without being sneaky or heavy-handed. If he swears or talks inappropriately, I can immediately take action. It's a different story when my daughter is chatting on the TTY or Instant Messaging (IM) online with her classmates. She gets rather annoyed when her mother and I look over her shoulder and often will try to hide things from us. Or if she's typing, she'll stop and try to send us on our way.

At first blush, it seems she's got a legitimate case. I know I hate it when someone is looking over my shoulder as I write. I once berated a guy at work who had the audacity to come into my office, stand behind me, and start reading aloud the e-mail message I was in the middle of typing. But am I being a good parent if I allow my child to use swear words or inappropriate language on a TTY? I don't think so. So I'm conflicted.

Eavesdropping is a big temptation with a TTY, because you don't have to be standing over a child's shoulder to have access to her conversation. If you wait until the call is over and the child has left the room, you can simply go to the TTY and scroll back the entire conversation, which has been saved in the memory of the device.

I feel uncomfortable doing this, because now I have access to more information than I do with my son. When he is chatting on the phone, I can only access half of the conversation. With the TTY memory, I have access to both sides of the conversation, and it kind of feels like I'm invading the caller's privacy, as well as my daughter's. As a parent, I can justify my motive, but it just doesn't sit right with me. Still, I continue to sneak peeks at the TTY after Miranda's conversations and check on the content. I guess my philosophy is "Better sneaky than sorry."

Deaf Girls Play on a Hearing Soccer Team

For five straight years, Miranda played in the Fremont Youth Soccer League (FYSL). For the first four seasons, her coaches were deaf men (fathers), and her teammates were predominately deaf or children of deaf parents. For the most part, she's enjoyed the organized soccer experience and having teammates and a coach with whom she could communicate.

However, in the fall of 2001, when no deaf dad was able to coach, "the deaf team" was broken up. Miranda and her three deaf friends were assigned to the Angels, a team with two hearing coaches and thirteen hearing girls.

Initially, I had many concerns about how this new arrangement was going to work out. How would our deaf girls fare in a very "hearing" environment? Would the coaches get frustrated with their inability to communicate or with the limited coaching they could do with the deaf girls?

I decided to volunteer to be the deaf girls' coach and to try to interpret as best I could what the other coaches wanted to communicate. I hoped that some relationships could be formed among the deaf girls and some of the hearing girls. I really wanted this to be a good experience for everyone involved.

I didn't have any illusions about being a great coach. I played some soccer in high school, but that was a long time ago, and I certainly didn't get beyond the novice level of play. Furthermore, I knew from experience that coaching (or teaching) is not my forte. I'm a good student, but a lousy teacher. I don't have the skill, patience, or flexibility to teach, and I knew this coaching assistant position would really challenge my weaknesses. I hoped I could pull this chore off without embarrassing myself or making the experience miserable for the girls.

I am happy to report that we were all successful. Of course, there was a learning curve, and at first, there was some awkwardness between the girls. Both coaches, Alan Cerro and Casey Martin, were upbeat and patient as we all got used to the routine of practices and playing together.

I was delighted to see that some of the hearing girls already knew a few signs and, in fact, almost all the girls knew the manual alphabet and were able to fingerspell their names at the first practice. One teammate, in particular, was keen on communicating with the girls. Her name was Melissa, and at each practice, she arrived having learned more signs. The deaf girls really loved her willingness to reach out to them. Once they asked Melissa if she wished she were deaf, too. This sweetheart of a girl thought for a second and said, with the smile of a future diplomat, "Sometimes."

Almost all the girls learned to sign STOP! This is a key sign, as our deaf girls would not be able to hear a referee's whistle. The coaches and hearing girls used a marker board and gestures to communicate with the deaf girls when I or other parents weren't on hand to "interpret."

The Angels started slowly with some losses and a tie

Nine-year-old Miranda dribbles the soccer ball on her Running Oranges team, which was made up of deaf girls and hearing girls with deaf parents.

but ended their ten-game season by winning four out of the last five matches to finish with a 5-4-1 record. They were a great group of girls! They really came together and gelled as a team. It was lovely to see.

The best feedback I got that season was from the mother of a couple of hearing daughters on the team who said she really appreciated having the deaf girls on the team and that her daughters really learned a lot playing with them.

The benefits from this kind of interaction between Deaf and hearing community members cannot be underestimated. These hearing girls and their parents are going to be much better informed about deaf issues and receptive to deaf people down the road. And who knows, some of these girls may some day become sign language students and interpreters, simply because this initial exposure to deafness was such a positive experience.

I believe the more exposure the greater community has to our deaf children, the more accessible that community will become for them. I would encourage parents of deaf children to get their children more involved in the greater community, if they are not already doing so. There are significant benefits both in the short term as well as the long term.

Deaf Actor/Director Troy Kotsur Directs the CSDF Spring Play

The California School for the Deaf (CSDF) at Fremont has a long and rich tradition of theatrical productions. All the CSDF productions are performed in American Sign Language (ASL) and voice-interpreted for the hearing for public performances. In recent years, CSDF has been hiring Deaf theatre professionals to direct the plays, giving students a real sense of professional staging and a role model to observe in action.

Some graduates of the school have gone on to professional careers in the performing arts. Hedy Ukovich Stern's daughter, Shoshannah Stern from the class of 1998, made her national TV debut as a guest star on the WB sitcom *Off Centre* in 2002. She has since been in several other TV programs, including *ER*, *The Division*, and *Providence;* she's also appeared as a regular cast member of a short-lived ABC prime time show called *Threat Matrix*. It's hard to believe that this is the same attractive young lady I saw playing the female lead in CSDF's 1998 production of *Romeo and Juliet.*

In March of 2002, I met and interviewed Troy Kotsur, a professional actor/director from Los Angeles's award-winning Deaf West Theatre, for a freelance article I was writing. He was on campus to direct CSDF's spring production of *The Three Musketeers, All Swash, No Buckle* by Pat Cook. It was a liberal and comical adaptation of the classic tale of French swordsmen during the Renaissance.

Troy Kotsur attended Gallaudet University before becoming a mainstay and award-winning actor at the Deaf West Theatre. *The Three Musketeers* was Kotsur's eleventh directing assignment, but his first one with high school student actors. He told me that the biggest challenge working with the students is that they don't have a lot of experience and can only rehearse four days a week, three hours a night.

"I wanted to challenge myself and be a good role model. I wanted to share my experience with the students," said Kotsur. "I hope to see some of these kids ten years from now on stage when I'm over the hill. I'll be saying, 'Hey, I worked with that boy.'"

Since then, I have seen Troy Kotsur as an actor both on stage and on the small screen. He is very good. In a Deaf West Theatre Company touring production of Sam Shepard's *True West*, which visited the San Jose Repertory Theatre, Kotsur gave a terrific performance as the character Lee within a cast of mostly hearing actors.

Later, Troy was in Deaf West's *Big River*, a landmark production of the musical that went to Broadway in the summer of 2003, then toured nationally as well as internationally. The show and Troy got great reviews in the *New York Times*. I had the good fortune of seeing the touring show in San Francisco with Brenda, Miranda, and a friend. We have also seen Kotsur act in the PAX Channel television show called *Sue Thomas, F.B.Eye*, starring his wife Deanne Bray.

The character of Sue Thomas is based on an oral deaf woman who worked for the Federal Bureau of Investigation for a time. Ms. Bray, the actress, was raised and educated in an oral environment, but also at the same time, which is rare even now, she embraced the Deaf community and sign language. Because the show uses ASL in their scenes and has subtitles to make the sign language dialogue accessible to hearing viewers, watching the deaf actors and the show is a rare treat for my daughter.

Ironically, *Sue Thomas, F.B.Eye* is filmed in Toronto, where Miranda was born and where we lived until relocating to northern California. While visiting Ontario in the summer of 2002, a casting director for the show approached us while we were eating dinner with our old babysitter Hao Wen Kong in a Greek restaurant on Danforth Avenue. As it happened, he was looking for a brown-eyed, ten-year-old blonde deaf actress, to play the Sue Thomas character as a little girl. Miranda fit the part except that she doesn't speak and no longer resided in Ontario. Hao Wen suggested they over dub the dialogue, and we said we could probably visit as often as would be needed for filming. We gave the casting director our contact information, but we never heard from him. Oh, well, film stardom will have to wait.

Ten-year-old Randi and her father in June 2001 at her graduation day from CSDF's elementary school.

Miranda and I met Deanne Bray at the matinee performance of *The Three Musketeers* a few months before, when Troy introduced us in the lobby. As many have said before, the television doesn't do her justice. She is attractive on TV, but gorgeous in real life, and really down to earth and sweet. I am proud that I have been able to introduce Randi to so many Deaf role models. She can't wait until she's in high school so she can act in the school plays. I can wait. The thought "She's growing up too fast..." has occurred to me more than once. It was hard to believe that my baby was graduating from elementary school and moving on to middle school.

Graduation

Graduation from elementary school is a big deal at CSDF. Randi and good friend Shea were the emcees of the graduation, which took place in the school's Little Theatre. Brenda and I were, of course, very proud of Miranda. She had more than held her own in the A classes and was maturing into a nice young lady. Awards were given out to students in different subjects, and though Randi did not receive an award, we were happy that she was moving on to the CSDF middle school with a lot of momentum and high expectations. She was excited and optimistic, too.

Chapter Thirteen
Middle School,
Break Out the Mascara

THE MIDDLE SCHOOL at the California School for the Deaf (CSDF) is aptly named as it sits between the elementary school and the high school. Its buildings have the same setup as the elementary school, with central pods surrounded by classrooms. The key difference is that there are lockers in the pod areas.

Miranda was excited to start sixth grade and join the seventh- and eighth-graders who stored their books and personal items in the lockers, changed classrooms, and had different teachers throughout the school day.

Robin Zane, an energetic hard of hearing woman, was the middle school principal. Ms. Zane was eager for parental involvement in the students' education and has always seemed to have a good idea of what was happening within her school.

One of the unique challenges for the CSDF middle school is incorporating the influx of new students who come to the deaf school from mainstream or small programs in their local school districts. Many of these new students find it will take time to become accepted by long-term CSDF students. It is the same as in a hearing school where it takes time for most of the new kids to fit in.

The middle school has a formal discipline program where students who misbehave in class receive LCs, which stands for "learning consequences." This euphemism for what we used to call "detention" means spending time after school in class with the teacher and missing any extracurricular activity scheduled for that day.

In addition to having an honor roll, in which students with good grades earn privileges, the middle school rewards students who behave well. Sixth-grader Randi, though not the most academic or the best-behaved student, managed to attend all the reward events.

Miranda marked her entry into middle school by adding makeup to her morning routine. Apparently, it is permissible to wear makeup in middle school. I was not too happy to see my little girl adding black mascara to her eyes, but at least she wasn't into wearing lipstick and blush, too. Just Clearasil and eye makeup seemed to be the only new additions to her routine. I did have flashbacks to when she was a two-year-old and demanding mascara cat whiskers every morning for months after Halloween. The daily application had just moved from cheeks to eyes.

Randi's preteen behavior and attitude change included new rules for her room, which were posted on her door for all to see:

Read This: My Room Rules
1. Only 3 time knocks. I will open door and you have to patient.
2. Not bother me!
3. If you knocks 3 time and I won't open door pls left me alone!
Thanks—Randi

My translation of the above is: "Don't bother knocking on my door; I will come out when I'm good and ready!"

The Roxy Gurlz

In the fall of 2002, Randi played on her first all-deaf athletic team. As I mentioned previously, Fremont has a strong youth soccer league that plays on the Central Park fields, which are just across Stevenson Boulevard from CSDF. A residential counselor and a deaf soccer mother coached a team made up of eighteen day and cottage students who called themselves the Roxy Gurlz.

Most of the girls who were day students had played during every season going back four or five years. The Fremont Youth Soccer League (FYSL) had always placed the deaf girls on the same team and added some hearing girls to fill out the roster. The FYSL allowed the team to play all their games during the week and scheduled none during the weekend, so that the residential students who lived far from Fremont would not have to miss games.

As most of the residential students had never played soccer before, it was difficult mixing and, unfortunately, the quality of play by the girls with experience dropped greatly. It was disheartening for me to see how much the girls who played the previous year had regressed. Playing with their less-experienced peers brought back all the bad habits of not passing the ball and bunching up on the field. I suppose this should have been expected.

What was surprising to me was how much the girls who had played before missed winning and being competitive. After nine games in a ten-game season, the Roxy Gurlz had a record of 0-8-1. The girls who hadn't played before were having fun, while the girls who had soccer experience were grumbling about losing. Both Randi and her longtime classmate and teammate, Shea, said at one time or another that they wished they were on a hearing team. After being reminded that on this team, they could communicate with all their teammates, they both admitted they preferred the Roxy Gurlz after all.

It was satisfying that the Roxy Gurlz finally won a game, the last one of the season, which sent them all away feeling good about the experience. Ironically, this was the only game I missed, because I was watching Terence's team play a soccer game at the same time.

Laid Off Again in Silicon Valley

At the start of the new school year, I was laid off from my marketing job at InnoMedia. I had been expecting it as there had been rumblings for some time with the economy turndown, and the company was far from profitable. Videophones using regular phone lines just weren't providing the quality that consumers expected, and certainly not the quality that businesses demanded. There were some genuine markets but none large enough to sustain a company that was only marginally interested in the field.

It actually was a relief when the axe fell on September 12, 2002. InnoMedia would have preferred to lay off people on September 11th; but this was the one-year anniversary of the terrorist tragedies, so they figured it would be more sensitive to wait a day. I found this laughable.

I would be out of work for the next year, but I had a severance package and some investments to fall back upon. I figured I wouldn't be unemployed forever, so I relaxed and focused on what I really wanted to do with my life. It was another palindrome year, 2002, so I thought maybe it was time for another big change in my life and career.

I treated the time like an open-ended sabbatical and joked with friends and family that if I got hit by a truck tomorrow, at least I enjoyed some retirement time. In between job interviews, I concentrated on writing.

Volunteering at CSDF

As time went by without landing steady, full-time employment, I felt the need to be more useful. I began to volunteer at the school's outreach department a few hours a day, before picking up my daughter at school. Though the wonderful Hedy Stern had moved with her husband Ron to Santa Fe, New Mexico, where he became a deaf school superintendent, I did enjoy working with the equally wonderful Bridgetta Bourne-Firl.

I enjoyed getting to know many of the people on staff at CSDF, particularly those in outreach. I did little assignments for Bridgetta, helping write press releases and contacting the media about newsworthy stories happening at the school. The school, and Bridgetta in particular, realized that it needed to raise CSDF's profile within the Fremont community. During times when lawmakers and bureaucrats are making decisions in Sacramento that adversely affect CSDF, the protests and voices of dissent seem to be heard more clearly when the local hearing community is supportive as well.

Bridgetta wanted the same kind of media coverage that the local high schools were getting and not the odd curio articles about the Deaf students that appeared every once in awhile. She and the school have been pretty successful in raising the profile of the school and the Deaf community in the Bay Area, especially in Fremont. Most every week, the local newspaper, the *Fremont Argus*, runs a story about some aspect of the school or the Deaf community. The *San Francisco Chronicle* and *San Jose Mercury News* organizations have also increased their coverage of Deaf events and the school's activities.

Three-Year Evaluation

During the early fall of her sixth-grade year of school, Miranda received an in-depth three-year evaluation by the CSDF's school psychologist and a diagnostic teacher. The summary from the report we received read:

> Miranda (Randi) Medugno is an 11 year 1 month old sixth grader at CSDF. This evaluation was done as part of her triennial review. Miranda has a documented profound hearing loss of unknown cause that was identified at age 17 months. She communicates via American Sign Language (ASL). During testing, Miranda was pleasant and motivated. Assessment results indicated nonverbal cognitive functioning in the high average range compared to age peers. Memory and symbolic reasoning were significant strengths in relation to Miranda's overall high average ability. While average with respect to peers, Miranda experienced relatively more difficulty on a task involving holistic visual reasoning. Current academic testing indicates second to third grade reading skills and sixth grade math skills. Miranda's written paragraph demonstrates continued progress in developing written English skills. There have been no concerns regarding her social-emotional development.

Needless to say, we were happy with everything on this report except for the reading level. We took their suggestions to heart on how to encourage improvement in literacy, but it was slow-going. However, in the past year or so, Randi has made a major breakthrough, and her reading is much improved. It's great to see her reading *Little House on the Prairie* and *Chicken Soup for the Teenage Soul* for her own enjoyment.

Brenda credits Nancy Brill's Reading Recovery program adapted for deaf students in CSDF's elementary school with igniting Miranda's interest in reading. According to the Reading Recovery Council of North

America's website (www.readingrecovery.org), "Reading Recovery is a highly effective short-term intervention of one-on-one tutoring for low-achieving first-graders.... Individual students receive a half-hour lesson each day for 12 to 20 weeks with a specially trained Reading Recovery teacher."

The Reading Recovery Lesson is described as:

- Reading familiar stories
- Reading a story that was read for the first time the day before
- Working with letters and/or words using magnetic letters
- Writing a story
- Assembling a cut-up story
- Introducing and reading a new book

Several years would pass before Miranda really got interested in reading and began doing it for pleasure. She enjoys scary books, and Brenda says that it was one book in particular that Miranda pushed her through that got her going. After that, Miranda began to have confidence in her own ability. She told me once that she envisions a movie in her head when she's reading.

I think closed captioning on TV is a big help in her acquiring vocabulary, as she frequently asks for the definitions of words she doesn't know.

Another Randi Christmas

For hearing people, Christmas is a time of beautiful music and singing. For Miranda, Christmas is not about the sounds of the season, it is about the sights and giving gifts! If I were still in the throes of dealing with Miranda's deafness, I would lament the fact that she will never be able to enjoy Christmas carols the way hearing folks do. Naturally, I struggled through that time when I could only think of things my daughter wouldn't be able to do or enjoy. I have no desire to return to those days of negativity. In addition to the sights, Miranda has always enjoyed the smells and tastes of Christmas. Most of all, she loves being with her family to celebrate the season.

Back when Miranda was three years old, I dressed up as Santa Claus. She figured out it was "Daddy" as soon as I walked through the doorway. Terence, a bright boy, two years older than Miranda, was fooled, even though he had my voice to aid him. Perhaps my way of signing couldn't be hidden from Miranda, even though I was wearing gloves.

When "Santa" began to bestow gifts on those gathered, I pulled my own wrapped box from the sack and gave it to Brenda so she could pass it on to "Richard" when he came back from his long winter's walk. Miranda would have none of it. She grabbed the present from Brenda and handed it back to me, signing DADDY.

That same Christmas of 1994, Miranda's cousins and brother Terence played musical instruments and sang songs while I videotaped. Each had their solo moment. Miranda insisted on having a turn. She sang a song made up of her limited vocalizations.

The result was not a beautiful song, though it was significantly easier to listen to than one nephew's trumpeting! Miranda enchanted us that Christmas day with her willingness to try without fear of failure. There wasn't a dry eye in the place. I will always remember this moment, when my child inspired me.

Subsequent holiday seasons with Miranda have been filled with memorable moments and good cheer. At Christmas 2002, Randi provided me with another cherished memory. After letting her circle the Target department store on her own with a plan to buy gifts for her family, she came back to me with a request for more money. She led me to the picture frames section and showed me a heavy metal frame that was being sold for $9.99. The frame was painted with the words "My Mommy Loves Me" in the ersatz style of a five-year-old. I hated shooting down Miranda's gift idea for her mother, but this was kitsch I knew Brenda wouldn't appreciate.

When I explained to Miranda that her mother would love the frame if she had made it herself, but wouldn't like this "fake" one, I felt like I was providing some expert parental advice about the value of things. Shortly thereafter, I felt like I'd been punched in the gut when she looked up sadly at me and reached into the bottom of her basket and pulled out a hidden picture frame that read "My Daddy Loves Me."

Well, there was obviously no backtracking and saying "I love it!" We just looked at each other for a moment. Then I laughed and hugged her. She smiled and put the frame back. I told her that the gifts that she had already bought for us were enough. We didn't need another one. She seemed both disappointed and relieved as she went off to buy something for her brother that she knew he'd like. As we left the store, I teased Miranda, saying that I had saved her about twenty bucks. She nodded and smiled again.

I suppose I learned again from my daughter that it's not the sounds or the sights of Christmas that are important, it's the spirit.

Grease–The Deaf Way Musical

I have been involved in many theatrical productions over the years. One of the most memorable experiences was my involvement in the CSDF's production of *Grease* in March 2003. I have functioned as a playwright, a critic, an actor/singer/dancer, a director, a producer, a stage manager, a lighting crew member, a stage hand, a ticket seller, a ticket taker, an usher, and even a reluctant puppeteer. To this theatrical resume, I added "voice interpreter for deaf actors."

I had always believed that one needed to be a certified ASL interpreter to voice for the student actors, but when I found out that the voice interpreters for CSDF shows used the play's script to support their voicing of the actors, I volunteered to put my drama degree and acting training to good use.

I thought it would be fun to sit in the front row and read the lines from the script into a microphone while the deaf actors signed. Piece of cake! Well, it was quite a bit more of a challenge than I had been prepared for. It takes immense concentration to follow the script, follow the actors, use my limited ASL receptive skills, and voice in character for multiple actors. At the end of each public performance, I had a splitting headache. Some of my voice interpreter colleagues were similarly afflicted, but most were not; I assume this was because they had more experience as sign language interpreters and teachers of the deaf.

Grease was the first musical ever done at CSDF. It was quite an experience. Now, of course, one wonders how do deaf actors perform a musical? Director Maureen Klusza's solution was to incorporate a karaoke machine with two television screens set close to the apron, facing the stage below the audience's sight lines. As musical numbers occurred during the show, the hearing audience heard the Broadway cast recording of the show while the actors signed the lyrics in ASL, using the words appearing on the TV screen as a guide to keep their signing in sync with the singing. Sometimes the songs and the signing ended at different times, but most often, they finished simultaneously.

I loved the experience and looked forward to being involved in future CSDF productions. It was great fun to watch the kids grab hold of the characters and the spirit of the 1950s. They bloomed into real performers.

Of course, I was delighted to hear that the show, which sold out all of its public performances weeks in advance, got good reviews from audience members. One evening, judges from the American Musical Theatre of San Jose high school program attended. It was very satisfying to hear that they commented favorably on the quality of the "professional" voice interpreters.

Another noteworthy thing about this production of *Grease* was that I had never seen a show improve so much from dress rehearsal to the first public performance. Literally, in twelve hours, the production team and performers pulled together and gelled. At their dress rehearsal, the action had to stop repeatedly for long periods of time because of shaky scene changes, technical issues, and missed cues by actors. By show time, they had put together a fluid, well-staged show. This is actually a common occurrence in the theatre—sometimes called "theatre magic," but I've never seen anything like this crew coming together. I really was amazed to see it happen right before my eyes. Director Maureen Klusza and producer Celia May Baldwin deserve a lot of applause for putting together, according to some who have seen them all, the most successful production to date in the school's history.

In subsequent productions, I have been the voice of the beast in "Beauty and the Beast" and Willy Wonka in "Charlie and the Chocolate Factory." The headaches dissipated as I relaxed and my receptive skills improved. My fellow "voicers," CSDF staffers Karen Lupo, Dave Keim, Terry Viall, Andrea Neblett, Laurie Guggenheim, and Tura Franzen, have been so supportive. We are like a little acting troupe that is never seen onstage and only heard once a year. We keep coming back because it is so much fun!

Miranda clowns as she hikes up the trail to Mission Peak, which overlooks the city of Fremont.

The Sound of Music

In the early 1970s, when I was about eleven years of age, my father took all of his kids to the cinema to see the movie *The Sound of Music*. (The Best Picture of 1965 had been re-released at that time.) I fell in love. I've had "a thing" for Julie Andrews ever since. Can anyone who has ever witnessed the opening shot of the Robert Wise film of Rodgers and Hammerstein's Broadway hit musical ever forget zooming in on the beautiful face of Julie Andrews, playing the carefree nun Maria, belting out the title song in the gorgeous, green Austrian Alps?

Obviously, I couldn't forget it. As testimony to my adoration of the movie and Julie Andrews, the first record album I ever bought with my own money was the soundtrack for *The Sound of Music*. Yes, it was one of "my favorite things," though as a teenager in the mid-1970s, this was not something I broadcasted.

Less than a decade later, on a tour of Europe, I got to visit Salzburg, the site of *The Sound of Music* story. I was in heaven—enchanted by the place. You can have overrated Paris, overpopulated London, and even historic Rome. I'll take stunning Salzburg.

Now, fast-forward a few decades and into the new millennium and imagine this father's delight as he discovers his eleven-year-old daughter's favorite movie is *The Sound of Music*. The fact that Miranda is deaf makes her selection of this movie musical even more surprising. Oh, I hear you saying, "Well, of course, she likes *The Sound of Music* because you've been feeding her positive propaganda about it since she was born."

Not so, I swear. There's no movie musical videotapes, soundtrack CDs, or movie posters in our home, much less any *Sound of Music* paraphernalia. She came across the movie on her own. It was on television one night and, similar to what happened to me so many years before, Randi became enchanted with the Von Trapp clan and their new nanny.

When I asked her why she liked this movie, Miranda was taciturn. You'd think I was asking her who the cutest boy in middle school was. Finally, after continued prodding, she gave up one nugget of *The Sound of Music*'s appeal to her: Gretel, the little girl. Yes, that little sister sure is cute.

I have a daydream. It goes like this: "Gee, maybe in a few years, CSDF will produce *The Sound of Music* starring Miranda Medugno as Maria von Trapp. What a nice vision." I enjoy this fantasy, because it is a possibility. And there are so many possibilities for Miranda that I never dreamed of when I first found out she was deaf over a decade ago. If I have learned anything over that time, it is to dream bigger. This is the same thing my friend Gary Malkowski says a teacher told him to do when he was limiting his own vision of the future.

As parents, we need to remove "they won't" or "they will never" or "they can't" from our dreams for our deaf children. Let's open all the doors and expect that our deaf children can do or experience anything they want. Let's encourage them to climb every mountain...

Epilogue

R ANDI COMPLETED HER FIRST year in middle school, experiencing some bumps in the road but earning some honors. Her poster for D.A.R.E. (drug abuse resistance education) won first prize and was featured on the program for their ceremony graduation. Her drawing depicts a young preteen, not unlike herself, in the center surrounded by thoughts of her future and a dialogue balloon from her mouth, saying "No drugs!"

From her science teacher, she received the Most Inquisitive Student award. Academically, she was on the principal's list again. She continued to struggle with English literacy but was determined to improve and remained extremely curious about the world around her and eager to learn new things.

At home, Randi and Terence have developed a special bond. They love each other very much and Terence

During a summer vacation to Canada in 2002, Randi (eleven) and Terence (thirteen) enjoy a moment together.

127

Two-year-old Miranda and I after a swim in my sister's backyard pool in San Diego in 1993. Photograph by Michele Medugno-Corkery.

communicates this with hugs, kisses, and signing. Oh, they still have blowouts and disputes, but it is normal teenage brother-sister stuff. I think it would make me nauseous if they were always lovey-dovey. That just wouldn't be normal. Needless to say, I am proud of them both.

Finishing up the sixth grade marked the halfway point in Miranda's primary education. If all goes according to plan, she will be graduating from CSDF in 2009, ready to pursue higher education. Allow me here to confess to a certain sadness at seeing my little girl at the threshold of womanhood. I miss the butterball who used to jump into my arms and play homemade games like "Who Touch First" and "Hide the Thing" (see Appendix A). I agree wholeheartedly with the philosophy found in a line from a James Taylor song that states: "The secret of life is enjoying the passage of time." Still, I think it's necessary to look back every once in a while so you can see how far one has come, which I suppose is what writing this book has been all about.

In closing, this is the message I want to convey to my daughter: Miranda, we've come a long way, baby.... And you still have a long way yet to go. I know you will succeed in life as long as you stay positive, are true to yourself, and never give up. I hope you will forgive me for being a stupid, hearing dad sometimes. I hope you will know that I NEVER wished for a daughter with ears that worked. To quote the lyric from another of my favorite songs that you'll never hear: "I love you just the way you are."

I hope all parents feel the same about their children, especially hearing parents of deaf children. They are incredible gifts to us and the world.

Appendix A

Games for Deaf and Hearing Kids to Play Together Successfully

A Workshop for IMPACT/Cal-Ed Conference, Sacramento–March 2002

With a little supervision and appropriate games, playtime can be successful, serving as an icebreaker and helping lay the groundwork for better and richer relationships between deaf and hearing children (siblings, relations, and neighbors).

Why is successful game-playing important? For deaf kids, it is an opportunity to interact with hearing kids within a structure and learn how to better communicate with the greater hearing world. For hearing kids, it's an opportunity to be exposed to kids that communicate in a different way and to pick up sign language naturally. It broadens their experience, perhaps making them more accepting of anyone that is "different" and teaches a different mode of communication. Game-playing between children who have different communication modes is an opportunity to be creative in conflict resolutions.

First things first: Parental involvement is a necessary component at the start. Parents can't just say, like my mother used to, "Go play!" With new hearing playmates, a parent needs to take the time to teach basic sign language signs (e. g., manual letters and numbers). Also, encourage your children to use pantomime. Parents can have chalkboards and chalk or paper and markers handy for the kids to use for pictures or words. We put up a chalkboard in our garage and tend to have some white boards scattered around the house to facilitate written communication as well as literary skills practice. Also, it's good to have sign language books for children handy—both for your house and to distribute to your deaf child's community (neighborhood or families).

We have found the following store-bought games successful in "deaf and hearing" situations: Candyland, Battleship, Racko!, Junior Scrabble, Yahtzee, Operation, Pictionary, Twister, checkers, billiards, chess, table tennis (ping pong), air hockey, foosball, and, of course, video games (though not all are appropriate).

Homemade or inexpensive games that our deaf daughter likes to play with her hearing family

Hide the Thing (for two or more players)

A game that's played with any small object that is hidden by one player while the others are in another room or in another part of the yard. With no speaking, searchers for the hidden object are given clues to the thing's location with the signing of HOT or COLD. Of course, the closer the searcher is to the object, the "hotter" they are.

Who Touch First? (for two or more players)

This can be an indoor or outdoor game, depending on the number of players. In this simple game, each player takes turns signing, WHO TOUCH FIRST (fill in the blank). So if one player signs, WHO TOUCH FIRST TABLE, the first one to touch the table gets to sign, WHO TOUCH FIRST next.

Hide-n-Seek

Everyone knows this classic game; no special accommodations are necessary for Deaf kids to enjoy playing this game with hearing kids.

Red Light/Green Light

In this game, one person plays the role of a stoplight and the other players position themselves a certain distance away from the "stoplight." When the stoplight person turns their back to the other players, this is "green light," and they all race towards the stoplight, hoping to be the first to touch the stoplight person before he or she turns around. When the stoplight person turns around, this is a "red light," and all the players moving forward must freeze. If the stoplight sees movement, he or she points at the mover, who must back up and return to the starting point, before the stoplight turns around for another "green light." The first player to touch the stoplight becomes the stoplight, and a new game commences.

Freeze Tag

Everyone knows this classic game of tag: The person who is "it" needs to freeze everyone in the game to win. The frozen can be unfrozen by the players not yet touched and frozen. The tagger's goal is to protect his or her frozen prey while tagging the remaining unfrozen players. No special accommodations are necessary for Deaf kids to enjoy playing this game with hearing kids.

Mirror

I sometimes call this the Lucy and Harpo game because it reminds me of the *I Love Lucy* episode where the two great comics mirrored each other. If more than two play this, it becomes the classic kid's game known as "Follow the Leader."

Puzzles (500- or 1,000-piece minimum)

Putting puzzles together, especially during the holidays with a lot of hearing relatives around, gives the deaf family member a place to interact on equal footing and engenders a cooperative attitude and group pride of accomplishment when the puzzle's completed.

Tabletop Football

To play, you need a tabletop and a piece of paper that is folded a few times into a triangle and taped. The triangle becomes the ball, and players take turns flicking the ball across the table, trying to score a touchdown, which involves getting the ball to hang over the edge of the table without going off. If a player flicks the ball off the table three times, his opponent can then attempt a field goal from mid-table. The field goal posts are made from fingers—index fingers tip to tip with thumbs pointed up. This game follows football scoring: A field goal is worth three points and touchdowns are worth six. As with football, when a player scores a touchdown, he or she may then "kick" a field goal for one extra point. Families can have holiday tournaments and crown a champion.

Speed (card game for two players; also known as "Spit")

To play this, you just need a regular deck of cards. Start by dealing out two stacks of five cards each, facedown. Then make two more stacks with one card, facedown. So at the center of the table, you should have four stacks placed in this order:

5-card stack   1-card stack   1-card stack   5-card stack

Deal out the remaining cards, dividing evenly between the two players. Each player takes five cards off their pile of these remaining cards. When both are ready, each player flips the 1-card stack faceup. The goal is to get rid of all your cards before your opponent, by placing them on a card in sequence, higher or lower than either card just turned. Each card is covered by a new card, but each must be laid down in sequence. For instance, if both a king and a 7 card are showing, I can play my queen or ace card on the king and my 6 or 8 card on the 7 card. The fastest player usually wins, hence the name Speed. When neither player can lay down any more cards, they go to the reserve pile and each flip a card and start laying down cards again until they are both stuck again or one wins.

War (classic card game for two players)

Divide a deck of playing cards in half, and then each player turns over his or her top card. The higher card wins the battle. If the cards are equal, then both parties throw three cards facedown and another faceup. The card of higher value wins the whole pot of cards on the table for this battle. These battles go on until one player loses all of his or her cards, which means the game goes on virtually forever. I think I've only once seen someone win a game by totally wiping out an opponent. Usually this game ends like a real war—both sides become exhausted and agree to call it quits.

Rock, Paper, Scissors, Hand Grenade (for two players)

This should be a natural game for deaf kids. Two players face off, each with one hand behind their backs. One counts, "1, 2, 3", and the players bring their hidden hand into view in the shape of one of the following: rock ("A" handshape), paper (flat palm), scissors ("V" handshape) and hand grenade (fist with thumb up). Rock beats scissors, scissors beats paper and hand grenade, paper beats rock, hand grenade beats rock and paper. Repeat as many times as agreed upon to arrive at a winner. Usually, two out of three determines a winner. But for the truly committed, or as a diversion for a long cross-country ride in the backseat, this game could go on awhile with "best out of 100" or "best out of 1,000" variations.

Two-Square or Four-Square

This is a traditional elementary school recess game. All you need is a bouncing ball, two squares painted on the cement ground, and three kids (or for bigger groups, four squares and five kids). A server starts the game by striking a big rubber ball into another player's square. That player must allow only one bounce of the ball in his or her square before returning it to the server (or another square if playing with four others). The game goes on until the ball bounces twice in a square or a player hits the ball out of a square all together. If the server errs, he or she is knocked out, and the other player moves into the recently vacated square and takes over the role of server, staying "king of the mountain" until he or she errs.

Hangman (word game)

All you need are two people, a piece of paper, and pencil (or chalkboard and chalk), and you're ready to play. One person has a mystery word in mind and then draws a horizontal line for each letter in the mystery word. Then the other player guesses letters (hopefully using the manual alphabet). For each wrong letter, a body part is drawn into a noose. When the "hung man" is fully rendered (usually head, eyes, nose, mouth, trunk, arms, and legs), the guesser loses the game. If the guesser gets the word correctly, he or she becomes the next mystery word writer.

Cartooning (creative cooperation game)

Grab a piece of paper and a pencil and draw three or four boxes aligned and attached to each other, as you'd see in a cartoon panel in the newspaper. Get the kids to create a character and a drawing of the character. Ask them to come up with a short story involving the two characters. Stress that the story has to have a beginning, middle, and end. Then have each child draw a part of the story in one of the boxes.

Fort-Building

Basically this is "mayhem in the den." Let the kids tear up the old couch, pull out the cushions, and toss pillows and stuffed animals back and forth. No real parental intervention is needed here except to make sure nothing and no one gets broken.

Party Games

"Musical" chairs using flashing lights

Set up chairs in a group and have one less chair for the number of kids playing. Then have them march in a circle around the chairs until someone flashes the room's lights. This is the signal that the "music" has stopped. The kids then try to find a seat. Whoever is unable to sit down is kicked out of the game; a chair is removed, and the marching around the chairs starts again. Repeat the process until you have a winner.

Uncle Spongehead (backyard summer day activity)

Get a big piece of cardboard and outline a large animal in pencil on it. We like to draw dinosaurs. Have the kids paint or color in the animal, then cut a hole where the head is located. Get the least-popular relative, usually a brother-in-law or uncle, to hold up the cardboard animal and stick his head through the hole. Get a bucket of water and sponges. Line the kids up about five feet away from the cardboard and let them throw water-soaked sponges at the head poking through.

Charades

Cut up some paper into small pieces. Write the names of Disney and other well-known characters on separate pieces of papers and drop them into a hat. One at a time, have a kid pick out a piece of paper from the hat. Each child needs to act out or portray the character on the piece of paper in front of the others. The first one to guess the correct character gets to come up and act out the next one. Parental interpreting may be needed for the hearing kids who are guessing, but encourage them to fingerspell and not yell out. Encourage the deaf kids to gesture and pantomime and not sign or fingerspell when they are acting out.

Costume Box, Props, and Mirrors

The easiest way to get kids out of your hair for a few hours is to throw them in the den or the garage with a box of old adult clothes and a mirror. Be sure to include all the necessary accessories: hats, gloves, purses, and shoes. Avoid scarves, necklaces, and ties unless you are going to be supervising.

Murder or Wink

From a deck of playing cards, take out an equal number of cards for the number of people playing, but include the ace of spades (the killer card). After dealing out all the cards, explain to the players that they are required to sit in a circle and keep their cards from the view of other players. The player dealt the ace of spades is the murderer, and he or she can kill the other players by winking at them; however, the murderer wants to do so without getting caught. The innocent victims must die without pointing the finger, and the remaining players need to figure out who the killer is, make an accusation, and get support from one other player before getting knocked off by the murderer. If the accusation is wrong, the accuser and the supporter die, and the killer goes on his or her merry way until everyone is dead and he or she is declared the winner. This game is very challenging when playing with deaf kids whose visual attention is, of course, exceptional.

Pantomime Game (The Machine)

This is an actor's game. For "The Machine," start out with two kids and tell them they are a machine, and each must perform a different repetitive action continuously. Get those two players going and add a new kid with a new motion every fifteen or thirty seconds, until all the kids who are in the machine are moving. Play with the machine by turning it up a notch or two, or slow it down to as slow as can be without stopping. If you have a video camera handy, you can record "The Machine" in motion. Then play back the tape for the kids for their complete enjoyment.

Dingo

Like Bingo but better. Play in groups of no more than four, and use a deck of cards for each group, dividing the fifty-two cards into four sets of thirteen. Each player gets a set of thirteen cards. For a group of less than four, put aside however many sets are unnecessary. Then have the Dingo leader shuffle his or her own deck, pull out a card, and show it. Anyone who has that same card, say an 8 of hearts, can remove their card from their active set. The winner is the first person to remove all thirteen cards and fingerspell "Dingo!"

Organized Team Sports That Work Well for Deaf Kids

1. Soccer
2. Bowling
3. Tennis
4. Volleyball
5. Basketball

(Always try to have at least one other deaf kid on the team.)

Appendix B

A Review of the Documentary Film
Sound and Fury

Versions of this piece ran in several different publications:
the *North County Times,* March 8, 2001,
and the *IMPACT Newsletter,* January 2001.

THE POWERFUL OSCAR-NOMINATED DOCUMENTARY *Sound and Fury,* directed by Josh Aronson, offers an opportunity to see both sides of an ancient debate concerning how best to raise a deaf child. The debate involves whether the child should use oral or manual language. There are very passionate proponents in both camps.

The cochlear implant, the deaf community, and one extended family are at the heart of the conflict in *Sound and Fury.* A high-tech device inserted into a deaf person's head, the cochlear implant stimulates the auditory nerve with signals sent from a receiver worn by the individual. This technology, both marvelous and cumbersome, has been successful in giving "hearing" to people who have gone deaf as adults. The controversy occurs when small, prelingual deaf children are implanted and prohibited from using sign language.

Many in the Deaf community, those who use sign language and consider it their natural form of communication, regard the implant as invasive and unnecessary. Community members are tightly knit and don't consider themselves disabled, but rather, different. They resent the hearing world's paternalistic attitude, and fear that implanting is not in the best interests of deaf children, putting them in a limbo state between the deaf and hearing worlds.

The human subjects of *Sound and Fury* are the Artinians, a Long Island, N.Y., middle-class clan, experiencing the remarkable misfortune of having the cochlear implant war waged within their family.

The film begins when the five-year-old deaf daughter of successful deaf parents Peter and Nita asks for a cochlear implant. We learn that Peter's hearing mother, a meddlesome, abrasive harpy, is fomenting the child's demand. Though the grandmother's intentions are good, she torments her deaf son's family, especially her confused daughter-in-law Nita, lobbying for the implant.

Chris, Peter's hearing brother, is married to a bitter CODA (child of deaf adults) named Mari. When Mari gives birth to twin boys, and they learn that one of the boys is deaf, they are devastated. The parents look to the medical community and not the Deaf community for support.

Mari's deaf parents are equally devastated when they learn of the possible implant for their grandson. It feels to them like a rejection of everything they are.

Sound and Fury is filled with intense, emotionally wrenching scenes. One of these shows Peter and Nita deciding not to implant Heather, then having to defend their decision to relatives who, ironically, refuse to listen. Another scene is at the hospital, where the extended family waits while Mari's baby is implanted. The film ends with the brothers accusing each other of child abuse—one for implanting, the other for not.

As the hearing father of a deaf daughter, who chooses not to implant his child, I can say with confidence that director Aronson has done an excellent job, giving everyone their fair shake and voicing of their position; though in the end, his film does seem to tilt the scales toward "the hearing world." Not surprising since he is a hearing man who knew nothing about the Deaf community or the issue until he started working on this film.

Clearly, the film needs more discussion about the quality of "hearing" one gets with a cochlear implant, which has been described by one implantee as "everyone sounds like Donald Duck." Also, more footage of Deaf cultural events is needed, such as an American Sign Language poetry contest. This would have helped balance the hearing world's frequent insistence that "we know better." As is though, *Sound and Fury* is a superior effort, offering both drama and education.

$\mathcal{A}ppendix\ C$
Resources

Book Recommendations

Bigger Dreams: A Two-Act Play about Deaf Politician Gary Malkowski
by Richard Medugno (Bloomington, Ind.: AuthorHouse, 2003. 144
pp. Paperback $12.50. ISBN 1-410725-37-5)

Hey, I have to plug my own work, right? I do think reading this
play about Gary's life will give parents and others a good idea of how
much a deaf person can overcome and how much they can achieve in
"the hearing world."

Deaf in America: Voices from a Culture by Carol Padden and Tom
Humphries (Cambridge: Harvard University Press, 1990. 144 pp.
Paperback $15.95. ISBN 0-674194-24-1)

This book helped me see the depth of Deaf culture and how the
Deaf community is not "just a bunch of people signing."

Train Go Sorry: Inside a Deaf World by Leah Hager Cohen (New York:
Vintage, 1995. 320 pp. Paperback $14.00. ISBN 0-679761-65-9)

The publishing information given for each title is for the edition that is currently in print. Some
books may have originally been published at an earlier date and by a different publisher. Also,
when both a hardcover and paperback edition of the same book were in print, I've chosen to give
the information for the paperback edition.

141

This is a memoir of a hearing woman who was raised at the Lexington School for the Deaf where her parents were educators of the deaf. Again, this is another peek at the Deaf community that will help hearing parents of deaf children understand what it is like to be deaf.

Seeing Voices: A Journey into the World of the Deaf by Oliver Sacks (New York: Vintage, 2000. 240 pp. Paperback $13.00. ISBN 0-375704-07-8)

This scholarly book by the famous physician who wrote *Awakenings* is surprisingly easy to read for the average nonscientist. I particularly enjoyed Sack's account of "the Gallaudet Revolution."

Deaf Like Me by Thomas S. Spradley and James P. Spradley (Washington, D.C.: Gallaudet University Press, 1985. 285 pp. Paperback $14.95. ISBN 0-930323-11-4)

This book, though dated, still resonates today with a story about how a young hearing family reacts to learning that their young child is deaf.

The Silent Garden: Raising Your Deaf Child (rev. ed.) by Paul W. Ogden (Washington, D.C.: Gallaudet University Press, 1996. 313 pp. Paperback $34.95. ISBN 1-563680-58-0)

This was, according to Dr. Ogden's website, "one of the first books to offer reassurance and answers to the torrent of questions asked by parents who had just learned that their child was deaf."

When the Mind Hears: A History of the Deaf by Harlan Lane (New York: Vintage, 1985. 560 pp. Paperback $22.70. ISBN 0-679720-23-5).

The Mask of Benevolence: Disabling the Deaf Community by Harlan Lane (San Diego: DawnSign, 1999. 334 pp. Paperback $11.95. ISBN 1-581210-09-4)

The first book is a history of the deaf, while the second is an indictment of how the hearing have "handicapped" deaf people over the years.

Deaf Heritage in Canada by Clifton F. Carbin (Whitby, Ontario: McGraw-Hill Ryerson, 1996. 622 pp. Hardcover $69.95. ISBN 0-075513-78-1)

This is an encyclopedia of Deaf activities and achievement in Canada. I'm hoping that some day when there's a new edition, my daughter will have a spot in this book.

The Eagle Soars to Enlightenment: An Illustrated History of the California

School for the Deaf by Kenneth W. Norton (Fremont: California School for the Deaf, 2000. 425 pp. Hardcover $25.00. ISBN 0-970585-60-8)
A history book about one of the finest deaf schools in the world.

Some of My Favorite Organizations and Websites

IMPACT
www.deafkids.org
IMPACT is a California statewide all-volunteer, nonprofit organization of parents, teachers, and professionals that serves deaf and hard of hearing children.

American Society for Deaf Children
www.deafchildren.org
The American Society for Deaf Children was founded in 1967 as a parent-helping-parent organization. Today, ASDC is a national, independent nonprofit organization whose purpose is providing support, encouragement, and information to families raising children who are deaf or hard of hearing.

California School for the Deaf, Fremont (a student-created and -maintained site)
www.csdf.k12.ca.us

Gallaudet University Laurent Clerc National Deaf Education Center
clerccenter.gallaudet.edu
Gallaudet University's Laurent Clerc National Deaf Education Center's Info to Go is a centralized source of information related to deafness, for persons from birth to age twenty-one. This includes education of deaf children, hearing loss, careers in the field of deafness, assistive devices and communication with deaf and hard of hearing people, the Americans with Disabilities Act and other legal considerations related to hearing loss, and employment of deaf and hard of hearing people.

Signews

www.signews.org

Signews is a national publication of the signing community that covers news, culture, youth, education, and sports.

Parent Links

www.parentlinks.org

Parent Links, a program of the California Coalition of Agencies Serving the Deaf and Hard of Hearing, Inc. is a state-wide network of parents supporting families of infants who have a hearing loss.